James & I & You
A Conversation with the Brother of Jesus

by

Mel Reed

Optimus Training *Publications*

James & I & You
A conversation with the Brother of Jesus
By Mel Reed

ISBN: 978-0-9894341-5-7

Optimus Training Publications
Fayetteville, Arkansas

Library of Congress Control Number: 2013911309

Introduction

A few years ago, I was offered a chance to go on a five day, life-changing Quest for Men. The idea was to reach the heart of God by rediscovering my own heart. One of the requirements was to read the Book of James. Not just to read it, but to read it every day for 30 days leading up to the start of this great adventure.

Reading this small book of the Bible (I mean, it's only five short chapters right?), I became a friend of James. His small letter contains some of the most powerful truths ever written. I have come to the conclusion that there is power in simplicity.

Some people read the Bible for historical content, and others read it out of obligation. They have heard that a good Christian will pray and read the Bible, which is true. But to read just out of duty? That somehow seems a very shallow process.

I and many other believers have come to realize that reading God's word, the Holy Bible, is a great way to "hear" from our Heavenly Father. Reading the word to hear, to grow, and to mature in Christ is truly a worthy endeavor. I did the required reading and study when I was in Bible school, and even though it was homework, I started to actually like it! The history, the stories, and the amazing miracles of God, made me glad to be a part of this bigger story. A part of history, - HIS-Story.

My pattern over the years has been to pray that truth will be revealed to my heart through the reading of the Word. That is my prayer for you, as well: that Father God speaks truth to your heart through this simple, but powerful, letter written by James. So let us seek the heart of God together.

James and I and You is not a deep, theological study of James. It is more of a friendly conversation between friends. Imagine that you and I are sitting with the brother of Jesus, and he wants to share some insights with us. He starts his conversation, and as we listen, we have some observations and comments.

That conversation should help us hear what the heavenly father is teaching us through this powerful letter. Do you get the picture? James, a servant of God and the brother of Jesus, is sharing with you and 𝗑. me

Read this book as a good conversation between friends, sharing insights and discussing in everyday terms how we feel and what we think about what our Father is saying to us.   me
Let's start this conversation with James & 𝗑& You.

James & I & You

JAMES
1:1 "A servant of God and the Lord Jesus Christ..."

Can I call myself a servant? And if I can, whom do I serve? My life since I was saved is not my own, even though there have been plenty of times I have still acted like it. Picture a slave who has been set free, but doesn't realize the chains have been removed! Still going through the motions of slavery, but free indeed. My goal is to serve the Lord God, each and every day, with all that I am and all that I am not.
As my friend James introduces you and I, let us take this journey together as we "discover and uncover" some exciting truths.

1:1 ...to the twelve tribes scattered among the nations, Greetings."

This is a reminder to us that we are a part of God's bigger picture. We have a rich history and a secure promise that God the Father told and retold, with his own lips and heart, to our very forefathers. So here we are, people of the twelve tribes, scattered among the nations. Wow!

TRIALS AND TEMPTATIONS

1:2-3 *"Consider it pure joy, my brothers, whenever you face trails of many kinds, because you know that the testing of your faith develops perseverance."*

OK, so these trials we are facing right now are actually a test. They are actually a test of our faith. James is telling us to "consider it pure joy." Well, I for one have felt pure joy, and for some reason it did not feel like these trials. How about you? This life here on earth will be filled with trials, tribulations, and temptations. I guess the "joy" comes when we realize that we must have faith for it to be tested in the first place, and that we must have faith to pass the test.

I remember when I was in college. I studied hard for the tests. I wanted to know the material so well that when I was handed the test, there were very few surprises. I approached it with confidence. I really wanted to pass. Maybe, here in the book of James, this same concept is found. Our faith needs to undergo the tests, and it needs to be examined to make sure it is strong. To prove it is true.

This is one test that you cannot cheat on. The only way to pass this test is to study, to be prepared for any question that might be on the test. Sometimes

life is a multiple choice test, and sometimes it can be a TRUE or FALSE examination of your faith! Do you REALLY believe that what you believe is really REAL?
Or are you living the FALSE concepts that the world promotes? We need to make sure we study the text book, the Bible, and put in the time and effort to grow deep.

When we ask for it, we even get a one-on-one tutoring session with the instructor (prayer). We also need to be careful not to cut class (the local body of believers) or the lecture (the sermon), thinking they are not important. For a well-rounded education, you have to be on campus (be present), and you need good interaction with the student body (other believers), agreed?

It is here that we prepare ourselves for the testing of our faith. Knowing the trails will come, time and time again, we must endure, remembering that we are developing perseverance. No one else can do the work for us. No one else can take the test for us. I can't take your test and you cannot take mine! Tell you what, I commit to you to strive for a 4.0. Will you commit to doing your absolute best? Let's do this thing together. Let's pass the testing of our faith.

1:4 *"Perseverance must finish its work so that you may be mature and complete, not lacking anything."*

So, once we are tested, our faith grows stronger
and yet stronger. We persevere, and hopefully we
do not make the same mistake twice once we have
begun to mature in the Lord. Look at it this way:
through this process we become more complete
and more mature in Christ. When we mature, we
are able to handle the "meat" of the Word and not
just the "milk."

Father God allows you and I to be tested in order to
grow in faith and maturity, and when we show
ourselves approved, we are given even greater
assignments. We are given more fulfilling direction
in His Kingdom. But what if we fail? Or better yet,
what do we do *when* we most certainly *will* fail. You
know as well as I do- we *will* fail. But God does not
want us to stop or to be discouraged.

Remember, James says that God is growing us to
maturity. He is a loving Father who wants his kids to
grow up, to mature, and to become more and more
like him. He continues to grow us, encourage us,
walk with us, and guide us. He will never leave us,
nor forsake us. We need to realize this. No matter
who has left us in the past, our Father is in this for
the long haul, as in eternity! He is here to help us,
grow us, test us, and to develop maturity within us,
so that we may be made complete in Him. Do you
feel complete? Completely sanctified, true, and full
of peace? I'll admit it: I don't. I mean, things are OK,
but it feels like there is still more to be
accomplished. It is as if something is missing, like a

piece to the puzzle. Does that make sense? Maybe that is the way life here on earth is, until we graduate to the next phase. Until heaven, perhaps we will not be totally satisfied. In our flesh we strive for completeness. When our friend James says, "... ***not lacking anything,"*** our hearts cry out, "I want that!" How free would we be if we felt complete and lacking for nothing? Lacking for nothing- you know, at the heart level.

Think about it. James is not talking about stuff. When we were children, we played with childish things. But now, as adults, we must realize we need to put away those childlike things, and be who God created us to be.

When we come to realize that, the stuff, the cars, the houses, the boats, and the bikes are revealed to be nothing but mere distractions. In going deeper, we begin to understand that we truly have everything we need. We must realize God's great love, and take this one day at a time. Day by day, step by step, in Jesus Christ.

1:5 "If any of you lacks wisdom, he should ask God, who gives generously to all without finding fault, and it will be given to him."

1:6 *"But when he asks, he must believe and not doubt, because he who doubts, is like a wave on the sea, blown and tossed by the wind."*

Wait a minute; James just told us, in 1:4, that we would "not lack anything..." Now, he mentions in verse 5 that, "If any of you lacks wisdom…" My guess is that most of us lack wisdom. At least, from Gods perspective,

Do you remember a guy named Solomon? In ***1 Kings 3***, Solomon asks God for wisdom! He was in Gibeon, and the Lord appeared to him in a night dream. God had said to him, ***"Ask for whatever you want me to give you."*** Solomon's' response was, ***"So give your servant a discerning heart to govern your people and to distinguish right from wrong."***

This pleased God, since Solomon could have asked for anything: riches, long life, or death for his enemies. God gives him what he asked for- a "discerning heart"- and he throws in some other cool stuff, too, like riches and honor. God said, "You will have no equal among kings in your lifetime." Wow, what a mighty God!

If we ask for wisdom to discern, which we so desperately need in order to serve God effectively, he will give to us without finding fault. What he is saying is that we can ask God for wisdom. He

10

wants to give it to us generously. As he did for Solomon, he wants to do for us. The key is to check our motives. Why ask for wisdom? So we can appear to be the smartest person in the room?

The motive for wisdom should line up with the purpose that God has put in your heart. If we are asking for the discernment to lead people, to help people, or to be a person God can use…my guess is that he wants to do that for us. The motive plays a part in the receiving. If the motive is to feed our ego, I have a Dr. Phil question: "How's that working out for you?" But if we are asking for wisdom for the purposes of God, we must not doubt.

In verse 6, our friend James is saying that when we ask, we must believe and not doubt. If doubt is present we are like a wave on the sea, blown and tossed about. I don't know about you, but I do not like the idea of being "tossed" around like I have absolutely no say in the matter! I want the direction I am going to have meaning.

That is a fairly clear picture of unbelief and doubt. It is not "if" you ask; it is "when" you ask. So when you ask, ask in boldness, and in confidence, because you have already determined it is for the glory of the Father, and not for the glory of yourself. SO ASK. Ask in truth, and ask in confidence. Remember that fear and doubt, are tools of the enemy against your faith, against God's people. When we fear, it is normally brought on by internal struggles or external forces. Satan would want to keep you in the dark and not walking in the great light and greater love of our God. Satan wants you to live a life of dissatisfaction and misery, a life of hopelessness, a life lived for you, and a life filled with the lie that it is all about you! He wants you to live a defeated ungrateful, unfocused, and uncaring life! Today, you and I have a choice. Let us choose life, a life full. Let's take James at his word, ask for wisdom, and pray to our Father for right motive, clarity, and simplicity. Ask with the right motive. We need to believe in the power and majesty of the Creator of the Universe, who loves us and who is ready and willing to give us what we ask for.

1:7 *"That man should not think he will receive anything from the Lord,*

1:8 *"he is a double minded man, unstable in all he does."*

Hold on, James, isn't that a bit harsh? But your point is made. God, our Father, wants us full of wisdom and he wants us single-minded. Notice what he said "single-minded" and not "simple-minded."

In other words, he wants us focused on the kingdom and seeking the will of God in confidence, knowing in our hearts that our Father has supplied a once-and-for-all sacrifice for our sin.

He has given us his one and only son, Jesus, to die for our sin. We can now walk with God; we can enter into his presence. It is by amazing grace that you and I, with our filthy sin, are made new and washed as white as a fresh snow high in the Rockies!

When we are single-minded and kingdom minded, all things are possible. He goes on to say that, if we are double-minded, we are unstable in all that we do.

Look around. Does it not look like the whole world has gone mad? This age is defiantly unstable. Could it be that double-minded men are making double-minded decisions? That may help explain much of the world's trouble. Knowing this, you and I need to be about our father's business. If we are not, James says, why should we receive anything from the Lord?

   1:9-10 "The brother in humble circumstances ought to take pride in his high position, (10) "But the one who is rich should take pride in his low position, because he will pass away like a wild flower."

Have you ever heard anyone say, 'Don't think too highly of yourself"? For me, it was, "Hey boy, don't get above your raising." When James says to us to "take pride in our high position," our humble circumstance, I hear him saying: no matter where you are in life, hold your head high. Do not put your noses in the air, but keep your chin up. You are a child of the king.

Being rich as the world measures richness means nothing. A man can have all the wealth, power, and riches of the earth, but if he does not use these for the kingdom of God, just what good are they? This man and his riches will pass away like a wildflower in the sun. Hum, think about that. Pick a flower, and see how long it will last without water? The idea here is that the riches of the world will not last, so don't think too much about such things. Again, be a single-minded man, for our time here is short.

Recently, my wife, who loves to read, was reading two books at the same time: David Platt's **Radical** and the book **Secrets of the Millionaire Mind** by T Harv Eker. Talk about a conflict. Platt's book is (basically) the premise of selling everything and giving to the kingdom, just as they did in the early church of Acts. Eker's title speaks for itself. As she read she, became conflicted. Of course, as the spiritual leader of our home, I offered the following advice: "Pray about it".

How many times do we use this when we do not know what to say? In reality, it is good advice. She has since been on her first short-term missions trip to Romania, the purpose of which was to take the joy of Christmas to a group of Romanian orphans.

Those events in her life- the confusion about wealth and her involvement in a sacrificial mission trip- happened within a week's time. My advice: Pray about it!

The point is that God wants our heart, our feet, and hands to be used for His glory. Double-mindedness is confusing, and my Bible says confusion comes from the enemy. (Well, except for the times when God threw his enemies into confusion and had them kill each other.) When we pray, "Your will be done on earth as it is in heaven," we need to think about the words we are praying. His will, not yours, and certainly not mine.

1:11 *"For the sun rises with scorching heat and withers the plant; its blossom falls and its beauty is destroyed. In the same way the rich man will fade away even while he goes about his business."*

I have known men who were single-minded. I am sure you have, too. You know the guy who was so focused on the business that there was little time for faith and family? I am sure that James is not encouraging us in that direction. Most of these "successful" people do actually fade away, as they go about their business.

As the world measures success, they are very successful. But if they would only be caught up in the success mentality in their personal lives, the causality would be self, family, and precious time, for the sake of leaving a legacy for Christ.

I remember when someone once said, "*You are what you think about.*" If that were true back in high school, I would have been a girl! And even now, some of us would be a fish or a golf ball. Seriously, we were designed to bear His image. We are called to be children of the Most High God. Yes, being single-minded can bring us closer to the life we were meant to live: one life lived in the Father. This life is short; let's purpose to live each day with single-minded focus for our God.

1:12 *"Blessed is the man who perseveres under trial, because when he has stood the test, he will receive the crown of life that God has promised to those who love him."*

Throughout history, the "crown" has been very symbolic. There have been wars fought over the power of and loyalty to the crown. There are countless people who strive for a crown. In *1 Corinthians 9:25*, we read about how runners compete for a crown that will not last. If you remember the Olympics in Greece, the victor was given a crown made from olive branches. Was this the motivation? Were they motivated by a crown that would dry out over time and become as brittle as the bones of the runner in his old age? No, it was the praise, the recognition, and the loyalty to country that compelled these athletes.

The popularity was huge, and the perks were nice, but there were not millions of dollars in endorsements back then as there are today. Millions in wealth that would make a good athlete put integrity by the wayside to cheat for a first place finish.

Lance Armstrong, by all accounts, was good (maybe even great), but he let the desire to finish first cloud his judgment. Now and forever he will be remembered not for all the wins, but for the cheating. His is a sad example of a "win at all costs" mentality.

James tells us of a crown of life. He is painting a picture here; we are blessed when we persevere under trial. We gain the crown when we stand under the pressures of this life and pass the tests with integrity and honor for, and in, Christ. Get this picture: we run the race, and we get a crown that will not wither away. We get a crown from the king himself. It is a crown of LIFE, and on the appointed day, we will cast our crown at the feet of Jesus Christ.

1:13 *"When tempted, no one should say, "God is tempting me." For God cannot be tempted by evil, nor does he tempt anyone;"*

Ok, let's get this straight. God will not tempt us, *but* he will test us. Revisit verses *1:2-3.* We will have trials that test our faith. God will allow the testing of our faith, but he does not tempt us. Have you ever wondered why? Well, no one knows us better; he created us, and he gave us free will. He will not tempt us, but he allows it so we can overcome the temptations and grow our faith. So where does temptation come from? Glad you asked-

1:14 *"but each person is tempted when they are dragged away by their own evil desire and enticed."*

There we have it! Temptation is from our own evil desire! Think of it this way: there are many temptations in this world, and if your evil desires seek after any of them, you will find them. Temptation, whether it be a piece of chocolate cake, a drink, a strip club, or a great golf course, is experienced by everyone.

We can all be tempted by desires. Not all temptation is evil, but if it takes our focus off of the Lord or away from living in righteousness (remember.... single-minded), it can have unintended consequences that may lead to evil. Stay strong, and know our Father God will not tempt us.

1:15 *"Then, after desire has conceived, it gives birth to sin; and sin, when it is full-grown, gives birth to death."*

Sin leads to death! Many times it starts with what our brother James calls evil desires, which drag us away and entice us. I have seen many people become numb to the Spirit and begin to serve the flesh- good people who justify bad things because of desire. Think of a wife and mother who has an affair, because she desires love. Or a husband and father who is dragged into porn, because of a desire for adventure. But these same people, who desire to serve, love, and glorify God, can through Christ Jesus overcome temptation, redirect the desire to a godly endeavor, and experience life in a whole new way. Life and not death!

1:16-17 *"Don't be deceived, my dear brothers and sisters. (17) Every good and perfect gift is from above, coming down from the Father of the heavenly lights, who does not change like shifting shadows."*

Here is the warning: "Do not be deceived." How many times have you fallen for something that looked good on the surface- maybe a business deal that promises it *"just can't miss?"* Or a dream job, only to find out that, once you're in it, the dream job is really a nightmare, because there were a lot of things promised that just were not true?

Most of us have been deceived in one way or the other, unfortunately. James is saying, "Hey, watch it, pray it through. If it looks too good to be true, it most likely is." But the good and perfect gift is from above. Our father is steady and true, and he is not like a shifting shadow, which you can't trust from one moment to the next.

Have you ever been around someone who is solid? I mean, if they say something, you know it's true. If they commit to a project, it is going to get done. Well, our father is so much more than any man we have ever known. He is the great I AM. He wants to give you the very best – every good and perfect gift is from him. Yes, he controls the world and all things in the universe, all which is seen and unseen. But he has the time to love us far more than we can imagine, and he, as any good father does, wants the very best for us. He gave his one and only son Jesus for you, his best. And he keeps on giving – oh, what great love he has for you!

1:18"He chose to give us birth through the word of truth, that we might be a kind of first fruits of all he created."

Think of it like this: your life has been created, and you have been given breath by the word of truth. God cannot speak anything but truth. When he created the heavens and earth, the land and the sea, he spoke them into existence. And all these generations later, he chose to give us birth. You & I were born into the truth, from the truth of God's very word. From his heart we were created, to be first fruits of all he created. The first fruit is an offering to God. The first portion of your earnings- the tithe,

the first fruit of your labor- is given back to God. Make sense?

So, if we are a kind of first fruit, we are to be an offering to God. We are to give ourselves back to him totally. To the Creator, we owe everything. We are a kind of first fruit, holy to the Lord, because he chose to give us birth. So the question is, what are we giving back? How does the world know we have been given life by the very word of God the Father? Can they see whom we serve, in our deeds and actions?

1:19-20 *"My dear brothers and sisters, take note of this: Everyone should be quick to listen, slow to speak and slow to become angry, (20) because human anger does not produce the righteousness that God desires."*

You ever been around one of those? You know, the guy that is called a hot head, or a know it all? James is telling us here not to be one of those. He says, "Hey, take note, brother." In other words, this is important. Be quick to listen. Not, "be a quick listener" – be willing to hear someone out, and keep your mouth shut.

So many times, we want to be heard. I think many people say so much just to help validate that they actually are here on planet earth. They want to hear themselves talk. James is saying to listen.

Like, "Listen with both ears, "as my uncle used to say. Think before you speak. Really give it some thought, and then, if you have something worth saying, speak. I know I have been guilty of speaking too much, when I should listen more. I have more to work on. Of course, it seems like there is always more.

After we are encouraged to listen, think, and engage our mind & spirit before we speak, we are now faced with the challenge to be slow to anger! "Slow to Become Angry." Seriously? James has to tell us that? I guess so, because verse 20 really lays it out in black & white. My anger and your anger will not bring about the righteousness that God our Father wants us to walk in.

Let's take a look at this. When I think of Hitler and what he did to the Jews, I get mad and I feel sad, even though it was a generation ago. When 9-11 is mentioned, it still produces raw emotions in some and anger in others. After all, who would think that human beings could do such unmentionable things to other human beings?

School shootings, church burnings, my buddy's wife having an affair- all these things produce emotion in me, and, yes, they can get me angry. But if I react out of anger, and not out of love, I will miss the joy of righteousness that God wants me to walk in. We must realize that his joy is our strength.

We can have anger over the injustice in the world, but we cannot allow anger to have us. We are here as followers of Christ to help bring hope to a hurting and dying world. We must walk in the hope of Christ, leaving malice and anger behind. Let's walk in the righteousness that God desires for us. Make sense? "How do I do that," you ask? Well, our brother James will continue to share God's wisdom. Let's be quick to listen!

1:21 *"Therefore, get rid of all moral filth and the evil that is so prevalent and humbly accept the word planted in you, which can save you."*

When we are born again, there is a deposit placed in us. It is the word of truth, the gospel of our salvation. Christ, the hope of glory! James is telling us to get rid of the moral filth that will surely lead to death and the evil that will overwhelm us, if we allow it. But he also gives us the key to overcoming the moral struggle.

He says it's the power of the Holy Spirit. The Holy Spirit gives us insight. It is true. Just look around. Evil is everywhere and prevalent in this world. For us to overcome evil and expel the moral filth and corruption, we must humbly and gratefully accept the word, the power, and the victory in Jesus that has been planted in us.

When we allow the operation of God's word in us, we will be saved from a world of hurt. That, my friend, is the good news of the gospel. We have just been given insight to walking in the truth and victory. We need not settle for the lies that the world and the evil one try to get us to buy. What will you hear? The word of a liar or the word of the Truth Giver?

1:22 *"Do not merely listen to the word, and so deceive yourselves. Do what it says."*

Ok, Brother James, we listen to the Word, we go to church on Sunday, and we sometimes go even twice a week! Now, that's not enough? I think if we merely listen, we do deceive ourselves. It's like taking a bath. You can fill the tub, but if you just get a washrag wet from all that water and wash behind your ears, but never get in the tub, you are deceived. You didn't take a bath. You did not soak in the water, you did not immerse yourself in the water, and you are just as dirty as you were before you ran a whole tub of clean water. Well, except for behind your ears.

James is encouraging you and me to not just listen, but to also do what it says. Not just listen, but do. Think of it like this: you can just stare at the tub of water all day long, but to get wet, you need to jump in!

It's great that I go to a Bible-believing church and am fed the Word, but to do *what it says* means understanding the Word and reading it daily. We should not be deceived. The Bible, the Word of God, has been preserved for us. The power of the Word of God is the same today as when it was recorded. We must put into action what we know to do. Jump on in. The water is fine.

1:23-24 *"Anyone who listens to the word but does not do what it says is like someone who looks at his face in a mirror (24) and, after looking at himself, goes away and immediately forgets what he looks like."*

Have you ever left church and, by the time you are out of the parking lot, you don't remember what the message was about? I think that's happened to all of us. I remember asking our kids, a few years back when the kids were little, what children's church was about. After some thought, one of them said, "God," which made all of us laugh. From that time on, "God" became the only answer to the question. Yes, it's always about God, or at least it should be. James is saying that when you listen or read the Word, take it to the next step. Put action to the Word and actually do it! I like the example he uses about a man and a mirror.

Most guys shave every morning, and it is best done looking in a mirror. Saves some cuts that way! But we cover our faces with shaving cream, and what

we really are seeing is that shaving cream coming
off our face. We don't really see our face. Next
time you shave, take that layer off, and then lay the
razor down. Spend a couple minutes looking at
your face! Seriously, look at that reflection. Realize
that God has made you just the way you are. Look
into the eyes he has made. The nose that smells
good and bad, the lips that can either praise the
living God or tear down our neighbor – study your
face and do not forget that you were created for a
purpose.

The point is, when you know what you look like, you
realize that the true you is deeper than the image.
The true you is your heart that can't be seen. The
Word of God is the same way. Listening to it and
reading it is good, but follow through. Go deeper by
doing what it says. That is the encouragement we
get from our friend James. In the next verse he
gives us the key.

**1:25 "But whoever looks intently into the
perfect law that gives freedom, and
continues in it—not forgetting what they
have heard, but doing it—they will be
blessed in what they do."**

Look into the perfect law. There, you will find
freedom. James encourages us to "continue to do
this." Stay the course once you have looked into the
perfect law. Jesus has come. He has fulfilled the
law, he is perfect, and he went to the cross to set us

free – to give us true freedom. So, when we see that truth, we are set free. When we continue to choose this freedom, not forgetting, we will be blessed. We are a blessed people not because of what we have, but because of who we belong to. We are blessed because of who we are in Christ, and because He is in us. The next time you are tempted to ask, "Why is this bad thing happening," or, "Why don't I feel blessed," look into the perfect law! Jesus, has fulfilled the law, and Jesus changes everything.

1:26 *"Those who consider themselves religious and yet do not keep a tight rein on their tongues deceive themselves, and their religion is worthless."*

I am sure this is right. As a matter of fact, *religion* is one of the enemies of walking with our Father. Religion is man-made, but a deep, abiding relationship with Father God is lived out of our heart. Following the rules is a head thing, but following Christ is a heart thing? See the difference? James says that if you can't control what you say- if your words say one thing, but your actions are saying something else- you're deceiving yourself, and your religion is worthless. I agree. Religion can lead us away from the truth. Religion can destroy a person when it is intended to build people up. Wars can start, as witnessed in world history. People groups can be erased from the planet, and religious fanatics can do some crazy things in the name of religion.

Father God wants us, his people, to follow Christ. He wants us to use our words for good and to walk in a restored relationship with him. That, my friend, is much more than a religion.

1:27 *"Religion that God our Father accepts as pure and faultless is this: to look after orphans and widows in their distress and to keep oneself from being polluted by the world."*

James gives us a glimpse of the nature of God here. He says, "God our Father," showing us that God has grafted us into His family. His family is made of those who have believed in our hearts, those who walk in a relationship with him. His family will seek after his heart, not practice religion! Ok, here is what God will accept: put the needs of the "least of these," along with a pure heart, ahead of attempting to look good in the eyes of the world. What does he mean to "look after" the orphans and widows? Exactly that! To give where there is a need, to lessen the burden, and to be there in a time of distress.

Today, there are so many needs. With wars all over the world, it is hard to imagine the number of kids who have lost entire families to the fighting. Terrorists constantly promote murder as a way to get closer to their god. And the result is that many children are left behind. In the slums in India, the killing fields of Afghanistan, and all around the world, there are children in distress. There are widows who have lost everything.

You don't have to go halfway around the world to see or meet the needy. Just look across town, or right next door, where the divorce rate is at 50%. There are many, many kids who are in distress – foster kids number in the thousands after drugs or crime have messed up lives, destroyed families, and left a messy wake. Natural disasters and manmade mayhem can tear the fabric of mankind, and the only hope is Jesus.

You want to practice religion? There is plenty to practice on. What if we got before God and prayed what he would have us do? How would he have us look after orphans and widows? Remember, we are to ask for wisdom, to believe and not doubt, to consider it joy, and to be doers of the Word (not merely hearers of the Word)
...*"and to keep oneself from being polluted by the world."*

Ok, so there is more to pure religion. Faultless religion is more than caring for orphans and widows in their distress. It is partly focused on you, to keep you from being polluted by this world. CS Lewis said, *"Enemy – occupied territory---that is what this world is."* When we think about the fact that we are not of this world, but we are just passing through it, things are put in proper perspective. We were made with a purpose, created for wonderful dreams, and meant to glorify God with every breath. But this world, this enemy-occupied territory, and most people in it, will do everything possible to tear us down, to pollute what God the Father has made.

James encourages us to keep pure, walk in righteousness, and continue to practice our faultless religion, out of a wonderful relationship found only in Christ Jesus. When he says to keep ourselves from being polluted, it must mean that it is possible for us to NOT be polluted. It may be difficult to avoid the world's ways, but it is not impossible. There is temptation everywhere. Our world is upside-down: good is bad, bad is good, and keeping from being polluted may be a decision that must be made moment by moment. But it starts with making that decision now, right here. Say NO to the enemy, and say YES to Jesus. Then let your yes be yes, and let your NO be NO!

"The safest road to hell is a gradual one-the gentle slope, soft underfoot, without sudden turnings, without milestones, or without signpost." -CS Lewis

FAVORITSM FORBIDDEN

2:1 "My brothers and sisters, believers in our glorious Lord Jesus Christ must not show favoritism"

Why would we be reminded not to play favorites? Maybe because some of us do! We play worldly games in the church. We see no difference between the church, the body of Christ, and the world. As a matter of fact, some people say they go to church every week, meaning that they go to a building and join with other people in a church service. We are the church. We need to understand that church is not a building. It is a people, and we the people of the Church, are a vital part of what God is doing on the earth.

2:2 "Suppose a man comes into your meeting wearing a gold ring and fine clothes, and a poor man in filthy old clothes also comes in."

So far, so good, right? Sounds like everyone is welcome in the building the rich are welcome as well as the poor. But in reading here, James is giving us an example. Today we might say, "Suppose someone shows up driving a Lexus, and the family that gets out is dressed nice and clean with jewelry and hair done right. You know – and they smell good! But in the same parking lot, a beat up minivan pulls in, and the people that get out look unkempt and a little shabby. Both families are headed for the front door of the church! Now what?"

2:3-4 *"If you show special attention to the man wearing fine clothes and say, "Here's a good seat for you," but say to the poor man, "You stand there" or "Sit on the floor by my feet," (4) have you not discriminated among yourselves and become judges with evil thoughts?"*

Judges, with evil thoughts! That points out what we are told over and over in Scripture not to do – judge people. We are told that if we judge people, we will be judged. Maybe it's human nature to treat the fresh, clean people a little better. Exactly – it's human nature. But what are we to be doing in church? Are we not striving to develop a more Godly nature? I hope so, but that is not always the case. If you show up in that Lexus, you might just tithe more. You might be an asset and not a liability to the church. So, a place of honor is chosen for you, and you can sit your assets down right there. But if you show up in jeans and a t-shirt, just sit wherever you like. We must be careful not to judge.

It should be more than a slogan for a local church to post on the sign out front - *"Everyone Welcome."* I would like to see a sign out front that says, *"Everyone is Welcome here. We will not judge you. We will be here to help grow your faith, and, by the*

way, we don't want just your money. We want you."
That would be one heck of a big sign! The point is
that we better follow through and put actions to our
words. I think the next few verses will help us to
understand what James is saying about that to us.

**2:5 "Listen, my dear brothers and
sisters: Has not God chosen those who are
poor in the eyes of the world to be rich in
faith and to inherit the kingdom he
promised those who love him?"**

No amount of money, and no appearance of being
rich in the eyes of the world, should not change the
way we love as Christ loved us. But it does. Don't
believe it? If you dare, try a simple experiment.
Dress down the next time you go to church, or visit
other local body of believers. Take a month of
Sundays and dress down. Yes, I am serious. Visit
some of the area churches, and, on the fifth Sunday,
come back to your local church and observe. Check
the reactions of the people. The leadership, the
looks and the comments. Then, revisit those same
churches a few weeks later, dressed in your
Sunday best. Record the response of this visit, and
then compare. Is there much difference? I hope
there would not be.

Most of us don't need to go to that extent to know
the hard truth: people judge people. It's not right,
but we do it. Another example of this can be seen
during economic downturn. Many people have lost

much of their worldly wealth in the stock market, real estate, and other investments. Many have declared bankruptcy – the chances are that you or someone you know has been through it. Once the house and fancy cars are gone, many so-called "friends" seem to be too busy, quit coming around, or just plain ignore you. Point proven. Many people judge people from outward appearances, but God sees the heart.

God has promised his kingdom to those who love him. He takes those who, to a judging society, appear poor, and he makes them rich in faith! It is not about the amount of money you have; it is about how rich in faith you are. Regardless of your outward appearance or the balance in your checkbook, do you have a heart for God? Do you love for your brother and sister, and are you living each day out of a deep, rich faith that is acceptable to the Father? Are you living, loving, and leading for Christ? Are you living, loving, and leading for God, and are you following the leading and power of the spirit? This is how we overcome the world, even as we operate in enemy territory.

2:6-7 *"But you have dishonored the poor. Is it not the rich who are exploiting you? Are they not the ones who are dragging you into court? 7 Are they not the ones who are blaspheming the noble name of him to whom you belong? "*

We must watch our words and pay close attention to our actions. As ambassadors for Christ, we are always under the microscope. The world is watching, and we do not want to insult anyone by showing favoritism. And if we do show favoritism, we need to realize that we are insulting someone. In this case of favoring the wealthy, we are insulting the poor. James goes on to say that it is the rich who exploit, and maybe it is because they can buy the favor of some people. The point is that we don't need to be those people. Our hearts need to be filled with the love of God. For kings or for beggars- it should not matter.

Unfortunately, the rich may drag us into court and slander the noble name of the Lord, but we, my brothers, should not play a part in it. We must "guard our hearts," as we are encouraged to do in Philippians 4:7 and Proverbs 4:23: *"Above all else, guard your heart, for it is the wellspring of life."*

2:8"If you really keep the royal law found in Scripture, 'Love your neighbor as yourself, you are doing right.'"

In the royal law- or the golden rule- James reminds us that it is right to treat others with respect, with love, and with honor. When we keep the royal law, it really is a game changer. It is no longer all about us. Our focus becomes doing the right thing for our neighbor. And trust me, this human condition on planet earth is such that we could use anything possible to remind us that it is not about us! Our friend James reminds us.

2:9 *"But if you show favoritism, you sin and are convicted by the law as lawbreakers."*

Which law? Which law are we breaking by showing favoritism? We are breaking the royal law. When we treat others the way we would want to be treated, we keep the law, but (and it seems there is always a but) when we pick our favorites at work, at school, or at church, we become lawbreakers! The point is that we are no longer walking in grace and love- but, rather, in judgment- when we allow this to happen. I try to look at people the way Jesus would, and it changes everything. When you see everyone as a neighbor, it changes what you want, and it (many times) changes what you need. Love, acceptance, respect, dignity, and honor have the heart of God in them, you agree?

The test will come when we are in a situation in which we can either love a person, or not love them. Remember our brother James' encouragement to treat all people with love, even the ones we would say are unlovable. Our calling is to accept people who don't smell like us or look like us, and we are to treat them as we would like to be treated.

2:10 *"For whoever keeps the whole law and yet stumbles at just one point is guilty of breaking all of it."*

True. Here is one reason we had to have a savior. We needed Jesus, the Son of God, to come, to live, and to understand the human condition in a world of sin. We needed him to tell us and show us that there is not just a better way- there is a best way to overcome and experience victory!

Man was guilty of breaking the law, because no one could keep all of the law. It is a great idea to have rules to live by. But when no one can keep all of them, maybe another plan could work better. No, man couldn't keep just 10 of them. The 10 Commandments were given to us (see Deuteronomy 5) in order that they may benefit all mankind. The question is: who could keep them all?

Maybe that's why he recorded them twice. Deuteronomy 5 is the second time. Exodus 20 was the first time Moses laid it out for the people. The people needed the law, but did they keep the law? Did they ever misuse the name of the Lord? Did they keep the Sabbath holy, or did everyone honor their father and mother? Did they never steal, never lie, or never committed adultery? Of course, all we have to do is read the accounts of the Old Testament to see that the law was rarely kept. Oh, maybe a day or a month passed, and maybe just having the law made everyone try harder to be good. But trying and actually doing are two different things. If we stumble at just one point, we are guilty of breaking all of the law.

Thank God for his grace and mercy! Jesus lived and died on the cross to give us freedom. He died for the forgiveness of our sin, yours and mine, to set us free. He did not die to abolish the law, but to fulfill it.

2:11 "For he who said, 'You shall not commit adultery,' also said, 'You shall not murder.' If you do not commit adultery but do commit murder, you have become a lawbreaker.'"

DUH! By breaking the law at any point, we become lawbreakers. Have you ever not observed the Sabbath day by keeping it holy? Or have you ever stolen something? Are you sure? Well, so have I. We are lawbreakers. We are sinners in need of a savior. Thank God for his son, Jesus, who redeemed us and redeems us still!

2:12 "Speak and act as those who are going to be judged by the law that gives freedom"

2:13 "Because judgment without mercy will be shown to anyone who has not been merciful. Mercy triumphs over judgment."

Most of us live under mercy; we want to be forgiven, loved, and shown mercy when we have fallen short. When we speak and act in ways that require grace and mercy, we need to remember that our brothers and sisters need that, too. Our sons and daughters, our moms and dads, our husbands and wives all need mercy James is saying that, if we really want the mercy of a living, loving God- our Father- we need to show mercy to everyone in our lives.

As humans, our nature is one of judgment. We think we are always right, which means when people disagree with us, they are wrong. Trust me; there will always be people to tell you how wrong you are. There will be people who judge your every move. What's the encouragement? Don't be judgmental, no matter how "right" you think you are. I guess we are back to the royal rule (The Golden Rule). "Treat others the way you want to be treated."

Remember, if you judge and show no mercy, you will get what you give: judgment. But if you show much mercy, much mercy will be shown to you! God sees your heart. Let us walk in what James calls the law that gives freedom, the law of mercy, because mercy wins over judgment every time!

2:14 "What good is it, my brothers and sisters, if someone claims to have faith but has no deeds? Can such faith save them?"

This question can cause much discussion in a conversation. We hear someone say, "Once saved, always saved," or we hear someone else say, "To stay saved, you have to walk the straight and narrow." Read verse 14 again: if someone claims to have faith but has no deeds, can such faith save them? James's point: someone can claim to have faith, but, if it is real faith, won't we see deeds follow? We would hope that deeds and faith are twins that are always present together. James even gives us an example.

2:15 "Suppose a brother or a sister is without clothes and daily food."

When we are saved, the faith of Christ in us compels us, through the Holy Spirit, to action. Too many times, when we don't know what to do when faced with a need, problem, or situation, we say to that person, *"I'll pray about that."* Yes, that's action, but you better take time to pray about it if you make that confession. Otherwise, you end up a liar. Here is a suggestion: take time to pray with that person right then and there. It encourages them, there are two or more gathered before God, and you will not unintentionally forget.

I remember the first time I had someone pray for me out loud. It made me uncomfortable, but it also felt good to know someone was standing with me in agreement regarding that need. Then, I will never forget the first time I prayed for someone out loud. It was in their hospital room. I did not know what to say, but I trusted God to give me the right words-His words for the situation. I was obedient, and it worked out fine.

Today, if we are on the phone, I might ask, "How can I pray for you?" You better have a couple minutes before we hang up, because the chances are that we will end up praying to God for the situation.

If it is a physical need, and there are needs everywhere, we must allow our faith to rise up. We must be led by the Holy Spirit of a loving, living God to take action to overcome doubt, fear, and flesh. Our faith is a gift from a loving father. It is for all. Our gift back to him is a faith bigger than what we received in the first place. He wants us to give it away, to take action, and to let faith move us to meet the needs of all whom he allows us to come into contact with. In this way, he gets the glory. Oh, that we may see the need, meet the need, and give God *all* the glory!

2:16 "If one of you says to them, 'Go in peace; keep warm and well fed,' but does nothing about their physical needs, what good is it?"

Have you ever really looked at a person who holds a cardboard sign at a busy intersection? Most of us, if we look at all, try and read the words written on the sign and not the desperation written on the face of the man holding the sign. What do we do with such needs? The world is full of pain, hunger, and such desperation. What do we do?

James is making a case for the action that flows out of our faith. If we spend time with Jesus- intimate, one on one time with our friend and savior- praying for clear direction, and if we walk in the spirit, opportunity will come. We will see the need when our eyes are off of ourselves. We can look at a face and follow through to meet the need in faith.

Years ago, I would see a need like that, and I would give a few bucks. I now believe that it was more to lessen my own guilt than to actually help the person. I have learned to offer food instead of money for food. Let me use the following example: from time to time, I will give a $5-$10 gift certificate to McDonalds to someone who has a need for food. To my knowledge, beer or wine are not served at these types of establishments.

As a family, we have given clothing, coats, and shoes. We have given Christmas cards with money and a message of hope. Just last Christmas, my wife and I took three of our grandkids out on Christmas Eve. They had crafted ten Christmas cards with some very colorful markers and some printer paper for people with needs. They drew some very interesting pictures and wrote things like, *"Jesus Loves You, Merry Christmas."* We had our nine-, eight-, and three-year-old grandchildren really into the Christmas spirit.

We sought out people in need. If you seek ways to help, God will open the door. We drove to a part of town where we knew the need would be great. We were wondering if we were going to find ten people to give these special gifts to. The fact is, we could have had twice that many!

One of the people we found that day had been badly burned, and her face was disfigured. Had we known her before, we may not have recognized her. The kids rolled the window down, held out one of their special cards, and said, *"Merry Christmas, God Bless you."* The woman was excited to see the kids and then shared a special gift with us. She said, *"Hey, you want to see my puppy?"* She then held up one of the bags she was carrying, and out of that bag popped the cutest little puppy face you could imagine! Of course, the kids were excited, and, at that moment, we all shared in the true meaning of giving. One God-ordained moment and it is a memory that will never be forgotten. James is saying to look for those moments, meet the need, and pray for one another. It is part of eternity- the *here and now* part.

2:17 "In the same way, faith by itself, if it is not accompanied by action, is dead."
2:18 "But someone will say, 'You have faith; I have deeds.' Show me your faith without deeds, and I will show you my faith by my deeds."

Our brother James, once again, drives home the point. Don't just say that you believe and that you are a follower of Jesus. Show it through your actions. Let people see that Jesus Christ is alive and well within you. Remember that at the end of Matthew 28:16-20, there is what we call "The Great Commission." Jesus told his eleven disciples to *"Go,"* to go and make disciples of all nations.

Notice that there was to be action. That's the "go" part. Not just: "Believe, and make sure you are nice to your family." The point here is to take this gospel, this faith, and to do something with it. Make a statement by what you do and not by just what you say. Jesus set this up by saying, *"All Authority in Heaven and on Earth has been given to me. Therefore, Go".*

In other words: "Look, you guys. The Father has given me all authority. Now, I am passing it on to you, so you can make an impact in this earth and for eternity." Capisce?

These men all had faith, but what if they had not put the "GO" into action? Picture this: once Jesus said to go and make disciples of all nations, baptizing them in the name of the Father and of the Son and of the Holy Spirit, they had a choice. They could have gone their separate ways, or they could have stayed together and just enjoyed the fellowship of each other. Could they? Do you think they could have just sat around and not gone? They were given a mission: GO!

We, too, have been given that mission, the Great Commission. Look at it this way: *Come,* you have a *Mission,* a *"Commission."* Our faith compels us to act. The story of how these men took the faith and changed the world can be found in the Book of Acts.

I have not found the Book of "Not Doing" or the Book of "Never Mind," or even the book of "Sounds Like a Great Idea for Someone Else, but Not for Me." No, it is the Book of Acts. *ACTION.* Nowhere in the Old or New Testaments is there a place where God's people are not challenged to live out their faith by acting on it.

2:19 *"You believe that there is one God. Good! Even the demons believe that— and shudder."*

James makes the point that there is one God. He says that if you and I believe that, it is good for us, but it is nothing special. Some people may have faith in a number of gods, like the Greeks. But the truth is there is but one true God; he is known even by demons! Satan and his demons know there is one true God. They know that God is bigger and more powerful than all the kingdom of darkness combined, and they shudder. In other words, they "believe" in God's existence.

Many people, when asked, would say, "I believe there is a god," or, "I believe in God." Good, but how do we demonstrate a personal, living, and loving relationship with the one true God? How do we live our faith out loud? We live our faith out loud by our actions, by taking one day at a time and putting our faith into action. James, and I and you, will be known as God's people not only by what we say, but also by what we do.

2:20 "You foolish person, do you want evidence that faith without deeds is useless?"

Hold on there, James! Did you just call me a fool? Oh, I'm not a fool, but I can be foolish at times. The point is that it is foolish to think that true faith can exist without tangible deeds. True faith will produce action that shows our faith. James, then, says, *"Here, let me build a case."* He uses evidence that the men of that day would have known and understood.

2:21 "Was not our father Abraham considered righteous for what he did when he offered his son Isaac on the altar?"

Yes, but he grew into such faith. Remember, this is the same guy who, before he changed his name from "Abram" to "Abraham," once told his wife, on a trip to Egypt, some very hard things. *"I know what a beautiful women you are."* What a guy. So far, so good. *"So say you are my sister, so I may be treated well for your sake, and my life will be spared because of you."*

That seems a little creepy to me. What about you? Would you let your wife go to another man's house and let that guy think she is your sister? But that's what happened. And, because of that, the Lord inflicted serious disease on Pharaoh and his household. Read the story in Genesis 12. This guy is our evidence that faith without deeds is dead. Remember, Abram became Abraham in order to become, by the very hand of God, a father of many nations.

The testing of Abraham is found in Genesis 22. Abram grew in faith and became the father of many nations, "Abraham." His true faith was tested when he offered Isaac at the altar. We must also create a space for our faith to grow. Our "test" may not be offering up our children, but we need to know that our faith will be tested daily – inside and out.

2:22 *"You see that his faith and his actions were working together, and his faith was made complete by what he did."*

So the key for us to complete our faith is to do. OK, I got it! But do what? Here is the beauty of the Kingdom of God. Our Father has allowed so many avenues to serve him. To "Do" this thing called faith, he has placed in each of us talents and gifts for the very purpose of doing. You may be a gifted teacher or musician, but, if you do not teach or do not play, what happens to that gift? Nothing, as a matter of fact. I submit that the gift will be diminished over time with no doing! Faith is grown by doing – No Do, No Grow. Our faith must work together with what we do. Someone once said that we believers are like Jesus with skin on.

Hebrews 11:1 says, *"Now faith is being sure of what we hope for and certain of what we do not see."* It appears to me that, if we take the gift of faith that

we cannot see and allow God to move through us
(producing action working together with faith), the
results can be seen, and our faith grows. Put
another way: you can say that you are a follower of
Christ with your words, but *the world wants to see
what you say*. This only happens when you act on
the faith you have been given. It is a gift. Can you
see the wind? No. You can see the reaction to the
wind. Trees sway, dust clouds, water evaporates,
and kites fly. Those are reactions that let you know
wind is present. Today let the world know that you
are a follower of Christ by making apparent your
reaction to Christ in you, the *Hope of Glory*. Today...
We Do.

2:23 *"And the scripture was fulfilled that says, 'Abraham believed God, and it was credited to him as righteousness,' and he was called God's friend."*

Has anyone ever referred to you as a "friend of
God?" What a wonderful way to identify a person,
not just as a Christian, or a believer, but as a friend
of God. Yes, we can be a friend of the Creator of
the universe, friend to the maker of all that is seen
& unseen! A true believer believes that Father God
can be a friend. Some of us can say, "Yeah, my
Dad is my friend." Some of us never knew our
Fathers, and some of us wish we had not, but this
God whom we serve is so much more! We can call
him friend, and we can be known as his friend.

Ever had a friend ask you for a favor? What was
your response? Well, a true friend will say, *"Sure,*

whatever you want." A marginal friend will make an excuse and not be available to give a hand, or they will first ask, "What's in it for me?" Here is the issue: God is asking for those of us who walk in **faith** to give a hand, to be of use, and to really put action to our faith. Are you a friend of God? He is our friend. Abraham was a friend of God, and his life proved it!

2:24 "You see that a person is considered righteous by what they do and not by faith alone."

The grace and mercy of God are available for all who will come. Galatians 3:29 says, *"If you belong to Christ then you are Abraham's seed, heirs according to the promise."* Just before that, in Galatians 3:26, we are told, *"You are all sons of God through faith in Christ Jesus."* I am a son, justified by faith in Jesus, the Son of God. So we must see Christ not only as savior, but as friend and as big brother.

I want you to get the following picture: when I sin, I take it to Jesus. Jesus puts his arm around my neck, and he says, *"I know. I truly know you have sinned, and I know you feel bad about that. Remember, I know what sins feel like; I actually took them all upon me at the cross. I know, now let's go talk to Dad about this."* See that picture? Feel it? So, when we realize we are to live like a justified member of the family, appropriate actions will follow.

2:25 "In the same way, was not even Rahab the prostitute considered righteous for what she did when she gave lodging to the

spies and sent them off in a different direction?"

The whole story can be read in Joshua 2 – she saved herself and her family (household) by an Act of Righteousness. But, in Joshua 2:12, she says, "Now then, please swear to me by the Lord that you will show kindness to my family, because I have shown kindness to you." James is showing us examples of deeds that come out of our faith, and, while our faith never may be written about, we are, in a sense, writing a legacy in the pages of our own history: our families, our churches, and our communities. We are writing for those who follow to "see," as they walk the path of faith for their own lives.

2:26 "As the body without the spirit is dead, so faith without deeds is dead."

Well, there you have it. I think our brother James makes it clear how he feels about putting our faith to the test, making sure action follows belief. How about you? James has made me more aware and has challenged me. We need to *"show people what we say"* as we grow deeper in Christ Jesus and as our faith develops. Father God will test us and give us many opportunities to come through for his glory and for our growth.

TAMING THE TONGUE

3:1 *"Not many of you should become teachers, my fellow believers, because you know that we who teach will be judged more strictly."*

Years ago, I studied to become a teacher. I pursued an education degree: K-12, coaching football, track, driver's education, first aid, or whatever it took to get a job. I thought that what this world needs are more good teachers. Of course, hindsight allows me to have a different view of our educational system in America, and I wonder if I would have been a good teacher in the public schools.

Not being able to speak openly of the Love of God, his Son, Jesus, and the desire that all would come to know him might have produced more frustration than anything else in my life. But our brother James is not talking about classroom teachers. He is talking about teachers who handle the Word of God. The teachers he refers to when he says, *"Not many of you should become...,"* teach the Bible, the Father, the Son, and The Holy Spirit.

And, of course, teachers are *all of us*. Like it or not, we are teachers! We are held accountable "strictly," and we are judged, good or bad. So, we might as well teach truth. Our families are learning from us, because we are teaching. Someone once said that the greatest sermon you could ever *"preach" (or*

51

teach) is the life we live, so the question is, what are we teaching?

3:2 "We all stumble in many ways. Anyone who is never at fault in what they say is perfect, able to keep their whole body in check."

Here is how **The Message** conveys James 3:1-2

3 *¹⁻² Don't be in any rush to become a teacher, my friends. Teaching is highly responsible work. Teachers are held to the strictest standards. And none of us is perfectly qualified. We get it wrong nearly every time we open our mouths. If you could find someone whose speech was perfectly true, you'd have a perfect person, in perfect control of life.*

That is a big "if." *If you could find someone whose speech was perfect…* Well, let me ask you: have you never been at fault in what you say? I think James may be on to something here. When we speak, there are several things that can happen, and most of them could produce stumbling. We all stumble. Sometimes, we stumble over our own words, or we stumble over the words of others, including God's Word. Because of fear, doubt, and sin, we stumble.

I think the point is that we all stumble. If someone were able to say the perfect thing at the perfect time, never finding fault, his name would be Jesus! And, brother, that isn't me, and it isn't you. My mouth and my words, even though I try hard to speak only in love, get me into more trouble than I care to admit. James, our brother, is confirming what we already know. We are not perfect; anyone can see that, just by listening to us! The truth is, we are not perfect. And, as for "keeping our whole body in check," I am still working on that one, too.

3:3 *"When we put bits into the mouths of horses to make them obey us, we can turn the whole animal."*

How true is that! In football, have you ever seen a football player be tackled by his facemask? Oh, yeah- where the head goes, the body follows. Same with a horse. If you turn the head, the body follows. Until a horse is broken, trained and ready, you're not going to put a saddle on the back of that horse. To make that animal fulfill the purpose of a horse, steps must be taken to get the bit into the horse's mouth so that you can lead its body with its head.

We must tame what comes out of our mouths, and the best way to do that is by controlling what goes into our minds, spirits, and bodies. Remember the term "GIGO" - garbage in, garbage out. In order for all of God's people to glorify God in all we do, we must start examining what we allow to influence us on a daily basis.

James uses a couple of examples that we can all understand: the bit and the rudder. Let's pray for complete understanding, and let's allow the words of our brother to reach us right where we live. Take a look at his other example. The rudder is one of the most talked-about examples of obedience and training that we will ever see. It shows we should make a point to examine what we say and how we say it.

3:4 "Or take ships as an example. Although they are so large and are driven by strong winds, they are steered by a very small rudder wherever the pilot wants to go."

Of course, in the time that these scriptures were written, the large mast of ships could be seen for miles. It was an exciting spectacle to see a large sailing vessel come to port or anchor off the coast. They would drop the longboats to shuttle the crew and passengers to shore. Picture the magnitude of such an arrival. When you back track on the ship's journey, you will see what it took to bring that ship to the desired spot, and what it took to anchor it at that exact spot. Decisions were made to leave and set sail to another destination. Charts and maps were accumulated, a crew was assembled, and a smart captain hired several seasoned pilots to steer the ship with accuracy.

If a pilot never consulted the charts, the navigator, the maps, or the stars, that ship would have had little chance of reaching its destination and arriving safely in harbor. That small rudder became a very important part of the journey. But that pilot also was there to do the will of the captain. Imagine that same ship with the same crew and the same destination, but with one thing different. They go out to sea, and the rudder breaks. The ship is now at the mercy of the wind and the tide. Our thoughts, our actions, and our words will determine our destination. If our mouths get us into trouble, it may be due to a rudder problem.

3:5 "Likewise, the tongue is a small part of the body, but it makes great boasts. Consider what a great forest is set on fire by a small spark."

3:6 "The tongue also is a fire, a world of evil among the parts of the body. It corrupts the whole body, sets the whole course of one's life on fire, and is itself set on fire by hell."

Have you ever been around someone who boasts? Whenever they speak, it is always about them. Growing up, we called those who boast *"wind bags."* But now that I am an adult, I refer to them as, well ....*wind bags*! James gives us yet another example. For its size, the tongue sure packs a powerful punch. When he says that a great forest can be set on fire with a small spark, we visualize that. Wars have started because of a poor choice of words. The poor choice of words is usually followed by a bad choice of actions.

He says a "small spark." Heck, I have seen some people use their mouths like a blowtorch or a lightning bolt. Talk about starting a fire! We see the analogy here: the tongue is also a fire, a world of evil. After all, when we look back to Adam and Eve in the garden, we can see they had it all: great fellowship with the Father God, great food, and great water. Just think- it must have been better than any Disney movie setting, until words were exchanged with the serpent. The seed of doubt was planted by words, and those words led man to give it all up.

When James says, *"It corrupts the whole person,"* we must realize that words have meaning. When we speak, there are consequences to those words. Think of it this way. Our Father God created all that is seen and unseen. How? Through his words, he created. Look at Genesis 1. The first five words are *"In the beginning God created...."* Then, we read something that is critical to who we are and how we are to live our lives. We read, *"And God said."* He spoke everything into existence. He used his mouth and his tongue; he created everything, including man. Remember, he did say, *"Let us make man in our image, in our likeness."*

So, we see that we were created to create, and we use the same process that God used! We create with our words, and we create our circumstances very often by what we say. If we speak fear, we live in fear. Where we speak faith, we walk in faith. Of course, we will not speak anything that has not first been thought. Our minds formulate thoughts, and then we speak them forth. Thank God we don't have to say everything we are thinking! That, my friend, could lead to many fires and disasters.

Here's the point – you are created in God's image. You are what you think about, so be very, very careful what you allow access into your mind. What enters in will exit out. Whatever a man puts in will come out! Please be careful, my friend.

3:7 *"All kinds of animals, birds, reptiles and sea creatures are being tamed and have been tamed by mankind,"*

3:8 *"but no human being can tame the tongue. It is a restless evil, full of deadly poison."*

Well, I guess we know where Brother James stands regarding the "rudder" of man. Maybe you have met some of those folks who are full of deadly poison! I have. They are some of the most vile and uncomfortable people to be around. God can change even the most evil person into a humble servant, if that person will allow just one instant for the Holy Spirit to hit the target of their heart! God's presence drives darkness out because of his marvelous light. We need to make sure we have no "poison" left in us to spew forth, no matter how we feel or what someone else does to us!

3:9 *"With the tongue we praise our Lord and Father, and with it we curse human beings, who have been made in God's likeness."*

Why is this? Why do we allow hurtful, vile words to fly out of our mouths like bats fly out of a cave? Could it be that that kind of thing is all that is in us? Yes, if that's all we have allowed into our minds and hearts. Too many people spend Sunday morning worship service praising God, and then Monday mornings cursing circumstances or other people.

Think of it this way: you are given grace and mercy from a wonderful Father. He made you in his image to be a *blessed blessing* that carries hope to a needy, dying world. A world that is so removed from the original intent of man, and just as we are created to glorify God the Father, our enemy had an original intent when he enticed Eve to eat of the fruit. The original intent of mans- original sin (disobedience) - has, over the ages, brought down many good people of faith. Great men and women have fallen, their families left in shambles and end up living lives of desperation.

This is not God's design. This is a corrupt, selfish pattern established by the enemy. So, when we speak (when we create) the hurtful, slander, or lie, it sets in motion the continued work of Satan. We, with our tongue, become useful tools in the hand of the enemy of God. Oh, I know what you're thinking. *"I would never do that. I am a Christian. Really, I am."* Some of the most hurtful words that people hear are from the people they love the most. *"I want out. I don't love you anymore."* "I am going to leave *your church and start my own." "You're nothing, you never have been, and you never will be."* Just words? I hardly think so. These are attacks designed by the enemy to tear apart God's design and to continue the sin set forth since the beginning. But if you take these same statements and establish God's design and purpose, might they all sound different?

"I am staying. God put us together and will keep us together. I love you." "I am staying here to help you build this church. Together, God's plan will prevail." "You are special. God created you and you are such a blessing."

Remember the line from the 2009 novel by Kathryn Stockett, and the 2011 movie of the same title, "**The Help.**" The line goes this way: *"You is kind, you is smart, you is important."* If you stop and think about it, this is an example of how we can use our words to encourage someone. But we can also discourage with our words too.

James continues.

3:10 "Out of the same mouth come praise and cursing. My brothers and sisters, this should not be."

Again, we must realize who we belong to. We must use every step and every word to glorify him, the Lord Jesus. See that? James says, *"This should not be,"* we see truth. I think you and I would agree. No, it should not be. But far too often, it is. Remember, you are more likely to change the person who wears your skin than a person who is wearing someone else's.

It starts in our minds. Many times, we are too negative. We must get on our knees and pray it out. Pray for true change to take place!

3:11 "Can both fresh water and salt water flow from the same spring?"

Of course, we know the answer to this rhetorical question. No, no it can't. A couple years ago, my wife and I were in Mexico on a get-away to Cancun. My idea of a get-away is a mountain lodge, but my wife loves the beach, so there we were. I used the time mainly to write, while she spent time at the pool. But, one morning, I hiked to the spot where the resort took guests to snorkel. It was a great big pool of clear, deep and perfectly C-O-L-D fresh water.

I asked to take a kayak downriver to the ocean, but the attendant informed me, *"No, senor, you did not sign up for the kayak."* So I asked if I could use a mask and snorkel. *"Oh no, senor, you did not sign up for that either."* I wanted to inform him that I had hiked here and that I had just stumbled onto the pool of one of the three rivers that ran through the property. I wanted to inform him that I had absolutely no idea what I was doing or what to expect, but my Spanish was not that great. My ego was, though, so I just shook my head, said "ok," and watched. Then, I thought, *"Hey, I bet I could swim all the way to the ocean."* I asked if I could use one of the life jackets, knowing I did not "sign up" for one. To my surprise, they handed me a life jacket and said, *"Sí!"* I was off on a great adventure.

Floating downriver through mangrove overhangs and shaded areas of the river allowed me to think. Wow, how great is this? Boy, if the kids could see their dad now! Hum, I wonder if there are any alligators in this water? I enjoyed my float trip. As I made my way closer and closer to the ocean, there came a point where the fresh water I was in and the salt water from the ocean came together.

Reading what James has written reminds me of that float trip. The river represents the word of God, and the ocean represents the world. At some point, they will run together. They don't start in the same place, and they do not flow from the same spring.

Think of it this way, must realize that there is opportunity to bring fresh words of encouragement, or to bring salty speech that can sting a person's eyes and open wounds. It should not be that we use our tongues against God or against our brothers. We must make it our purpose to use our breath, our words, and our actions to glorify God the Father.

3:12 "My brothers and sisters, can a fig tree bear olives, or a grapevine bear figs? Neither can a salt spring produce fresh water."

Again, James tells us to realize our mouths will speak forth what we allow. You may strive for righteousness, but, if you pollute your minds with the things of the world or allow the enemy of your heart to gain a foothold, you will experience a flow of words that will be unintended and hurtful.

Tame the tongue? Of course, it is a lofty goal only to be accomplished when we win the battle in our minds. In the soul of man is a battlefield that rivals Gettysburg, Normandy, or Afghanistan. There in our minds, the battle is fought and won as a result of God's Holy Spirit living in us.

The Holy Spirit's work in our hearts can be, and usually is, a turning point in the battle. When our hearts are one with the Lord, the battle is won. To be one, is to win. When we see the manifestation of that victory and let our faith reign supreme over our flesh, that is when great and mighty things can be accomplished for the kingdom of God. Remember, faith without deeds is dead! We must build up our inner man – our spirit- to take charge over our minds if we are to have any chance of controlling our mouths or keeping our tongues tamed!

TWO KINDS OF WISDOM

3:13 "Who is wise and understanding among you? Let them show it by their good life, by deeds done in the humility that comes from wisdom."

I can truly say that wisdom and understanding are the two things I have prayed most for over the years. When James told *us to ask God for wisdom if we lack wisdom (1:5),* he promised it would be added to us. So I ask, and over the years there have been many right decisions made, due to the wisdom God has given me. But, of course, just the opposite is true when I don't use wisdom. When I make decisions out of the desire for selfish gain, it normally is a mess. But when the understanding comes from reading the Word of God and listening to that still, small voice, things go better.

What do you think? Being wise and understanding, and following the call and mission of God; will it always lead to a good life? That is where our deeds will make a difference in peoples' lives. Knowing much about a little, or knowing little about much, is not the same as wisdom.

People have confused knowledge and wisdom for generations.. Many learned men have had great knowledge. It is the knowledge that comes from books and constant study. But true wisdom comes from one book, the Bible, and our source, the Father, Son, and Holy Spirit.

So, in humility, we show this good life by deeds done to glorify God. When you give a cup of water to a thirsty soul in the name of Jesus, that deed will not go unnoticed. Oh, the world may never acknowledge it, but your Father in heaven does notice.

A knowledgeable man, a man full of facts may attempt to help a thirsty soul by describing the chemical properties of water. That man may say something along the lines of the following statement.

"Did you know that one molecule of water has two hydrogen atoms bonded to a single oxygen atom."

Or they might explain that the Earth's surface is 70% water, which makes it the most abundant compound on the planet. They might also mention that water makes up 55% to 78% of the human body, which may explain why you find yourself thirsty. Hum, still parched, and needing a drink!

A wise man understands and lets the deed flow from a compassionate heart. For instance, you meet a man who needs water. You say, *"Yes, friend, you are thirsty. Here, have a cup of water, drink."* See the difference? I'm sure you have met both kinds of people. I have.

So, let's be wise, filled with understanding and showing a lost and hurting world our good life in Christ. We can humbly make a difference every day we are here on Earth. Remember, it is not all about us. It is all for God's glory.

3:14 *"But if you harbor bitter envy and selfish ambition in your hearts, do not boast about it or deny the truth"*

James warns us regarding the world's structure. Operating out of selfish ambition or envy is dangerous. Doing everything for yourself is the shallowest life you could live. When every moment is consumed by thoughts of, "How can I get more for me," it opens the door for whatever means is necessary to accomplish that. Lying, stealing, cheating- no problem. The end justifies the means.

Keep in mind that the devil has always used this against man. Remember in the garden: Adam and

Eve were changed. They were deceived as men still are today. In *Genesis 3:4: "You will not surely die, the serpent said to the women (5) "For God knows when you eat of it, your eyes will be opened, and you will be like God, knowing good and evil."*

Her eyes were open. She was like God. She was created in his image, but the idea of gaining more for herself enticed her and Adam to eat. One thing Satan actually got right is, that man would *"know evil."* Mankind gave up so much to lose everything. Think about that statement, and let me repeat it. *Mankind gave up so much to lose everything.*

Until Jesus died as our ultimate sacrifice on the cross and restored us to God, we had no hope. Our "worldly wisdom" is not wise at all. Think of it as trash, garbage, and evil when held up to the true light of wisdom that can only come from God. It needs to be taken out and disposed of.

3:16 "For where you have envy and selfish ambition, there you find disorder and every evil practice."

I know in my life that when things are out of order, it allows for evil to reign, and not Christ. When evil is in charge because of my choices, evil practices lead in directions that are unnatural, unproductive, and damaging. Our families will suffer, our jobs will never be satisfying, and our Christian walk will never be all it is designed to be, if selfish ambition is allowed to linger. Not SELF ambition, SELFISH ambition, big difference, right?

Ambition is not a bad thing. We read all through scripture about how God gave man the privilege of work. When God's people are ambitious and work for God and his kingdom, good things happen. It's when we consider nothing but ourselves, when we do things just to satisfy ourselves, that we miss the mark. That is when disorder, evil, and sin grow. When we allow this, we will harvest a crop of death!

3:17 *"But the wisdom that comes from heaven is first of all pure; then peace-loving, considerate, submissive, full of mercy and good fruit, impartial and sincere."*

"Pure Wisdom" sounds like a great movie title. A movie that might be based on a village that seeks answers to all of life's questions, and it knows there is but one source. That source is the man from Heaven, the wise one; he will know, for he knows all things! The story line may be about all the people, their problems, issues and victories in life. Would you go see it? I would. But if we just look around, it appears we are living the script from this movie every day of our lives!

As a matter of fact, the source of pure wisdom truly is Heaven. The things mentioned by James in 3:17 can only be found when we seek the Son of God.

Pure, peace-loving, considerate, submissive, full of mercy – all of these are qualities we should strive for. These are found in Christ alone. Wisdom from heaven is considerate and submissive. We look at these words, and mostly we visualize meek, mild, and easy-to-be-around people. Wise people, wisdom knows where to be considerate, where to submit, and where to take a stand. We all need to pray for more mercy.

Read verse 16 again: we need to pray that God gives us *pure wisdom, so we can* walk out our faith and maximize the opportunity of the mission.

3:18 "Peacemakers who sow in peace reap a harvest of righteousness."

Wisdom-filled peacemakers who love peace will sow peace, and they will harvest righteousness. The same can be said for people who sow divisiveness or chaos.They will produce a crop of the same. Remember, *"Choose this day whom you will serve."* Do you agree that the choice is between God and the Devil, between right and wrong, and between good and evil? I do, and, while that's true, there is a third choice. We can choose to serve nothing. No one, zip, nadda, zero. Choosing nothing is another way of saying, "I have no convictions, I have no mission, and I don't care about the future." Choosing nothing is also a choice, an unfortunate choice, but a choice none the less. As a man thinks, so he is!

You can sow in fertile ground and produce a crop of whatever you plant. If you sow peace or hate, you will produce more of the same. If you sow no seed, you will grow absolutely nothing. You will have no harvest and no righteousness. Planting nothing, is what many people think this is the safest way to approach life. *"If I don't step out, no one can expect much from me."*

If we don't try, we will not fail. To those people who believe that, I say that you already have failed by not attempting anything of great value for God. Yes, you may feel safe for the moment, but your spirit will not soar to new heights. When you attempt and succeed, and end up accomplishing something for the kingdom of God. Your spirit soars!

When was the last time you did something that made you feel alive? We must not sit in our Christian boxes, on our Christian assets while the world continues to die. You want righteousness, plant a righteousness seed.

If you want peace, sow peace. If you want to experience God's very best, give him your very best. God is not a respecter of people; he gives his children, you and I, what we ask for by faith. But the motive must be to glorify him. Sowing and reaping have been going on since the beginning of man. God has put into place this universal law. *What you sow, you will reap.* Unfortunately, some men say, "I don't sow so that I don't have to weed my garden. Plus, this reaping thing sure sounds like a lot of work."

If we are not excited about waking up to see what opportunity God has for us today, then we need to change our seed or change the field in which we have sown. We may need to find a more fertile field. We are to produce a harvest – a crop for God.

Fear and doubt are two of the biggest things with which the enemy attacks the hearts of God's people. Listen, it is past time to get the fears and doubt out! We must operate and make decisions from the center of faith and wisdom, and it starts with asking our loving Father for both. Let's pray that right now.

Father, you know my heart. It is for you and your glory. I pray today for pure wisdom I pray for the boldness to step out in faith. Give me wisdom. Grow my faith so I may sow more and produce more, not for me but for your kingdom, Father. I thank you for the increase. May your kingdom, your righteousness, fill me to overflowing – in the mighty name of Jesus. Amen.

You may want to continue praying this prayer every morning until you see a difference in how you approach the day. The general consensus is that it takes 21-30 days to form a new habit. I trust it is worth a couple of minutes a day to pray this simple little prayer in order to produce change in your life. And, if you agree, please join a growing number of believers in praying together for WISDOM.

SUBMIT YOURSELF TO GOD

4:1 "What causes fights and quarrels among you? Don't they come from your desires that battle within you?"

Well, thanks James, that about sums it up! Our desires are at war. We want a _____(fill in the blank). Not necessarily need, but want. We desire to have money, a new house, a new car, and, for some people, a new spouse! We humans have learned, quite by accident that we are very capable of lying and cheating to get what we want. We will fight for it, and God help anyone who gets in our way.

We will argue and quarrel with whomever it takes to get our point of view accepted, because we are right! Or, so we think. This battle of desire is dangerous and can lead to sin. Most of the time, it does. Fights and quarrels are produced by ungodly desires.

4:2 *"You desire but do not have, so you kill. You covet but you cannot get what you want, so you quarrel and fight. You do not have because you do not ask God."*

Here is a truth for us to really grasp: we *do not have because we do not ask* God!

We think we can do it ourselves. We want something, so we go get it. When we can't have it, the frustration and unsettledness kicks in. We are instructed in *Matthew 7:7: "Ask and it will be given to you; seek and you will find; knock and the door will be opened for you."*

What does that say to you and me? James is pointing out that we do not ask God for what we need, but we listen to ourselves about what we

70

want! That, in my opinion, is the big difference between getting and getting frustrated. When we quit asking self and start asking God, we are put in the positive position to receive from God.

Think of it this way: you want something so bad, you are ready to fight for it. So, with clenched fists, you stand your ground. Or, you want something so much; you are willing to take your request to our Father. You humbly submit your will to his, and you ask. Then, with uplifted hands, you praise his holy name. Two postures, same request!

One, almost defiant: *I want this, clenched fist.*

The other: *Lord, you know what I need. I receive it, open hands.*

If our fists are clenched, ready for the fight, nothing can be placed in our hand. Try this right where you sit. Make a fist, and look at it. Where can you possibly receive a blessing? Now, open that same hand, palm up, and spread your fingers. Stretch them out as far as they can go. See that? That is where you will receive God's answer. You have just created capacity to receive, and you have surrendered your will to the Father's. He wants to give you what you ask for. Of course, as with any good father, if it is not good for us (if it will not lead to accomplishing our mission), he may withhold it.

The same is true with our hearts. We close them up, too. Have you ever heard that your heart is as big as your fist? It's true; the physical muscle that pumps blood throughout our body is about the size of our fists. When God takes hold of that heart in the spiritual realm, it opens up like your fist does. It becomes open and ready to receive what God has for you.

4:3 "When you ask, you do not receive, because you ask with wrong motives, that you may spend what you get on your pleasures."

Here again, we must seek the kingdom of Heaven and God's righteousness. When we ask while seeking, we ask in confidence. We ask with a right heart. Years ago I wanted to retire young. I wanted to retire so that I could enjoy myself. "Myself, yes, as in ME." Needless to say, my finances would not allow that to happen, and my Father in Heaven had other plans. How about you? Have you ever asked for something, or set a goal, and nothing happened?

Of course, that has happened to most of us, but we need to remember that it all comes down to motive. I usually ask, "How can this glorify God?" The word *glory* can be translated into "significance." God must be significant in our lives, for us to do anything significant while here on earth. When Jesus showed us how to pray, he said, *"Your kingdom come, your will be done."* With his motive lined up and identified up front, his and the Father's will were one.

You may say, "Well, of course they were. Jesus and the Father were always one, from the beginning of time. Of course Jesus got his prayers answered." Yes, but we must also remember that

Jesus was God and man. He is our example in every way. His prayers and his motives will always serve us well when followed. When we seek after our pleasures, and not the kingdom of God, we fool ourselves. And when we are deceived, bad things usually result.

Let me give you an example. When Jesus was on earth in the flesh, a man said to him, *"Teacher, I will follow you wherever you go."* (Matt. 8:19) Jesus responded, *"Foxes have holes, and birds have nests, but the son of man has no place to lay his head."* That was a true statement. It was also a statement that most lukewarm followers of Christ have a hard time hearing.

Here is God himself, in the flesh, saying, *"Hey, you want to follow me? I don't even have my own bed."* Of course, God can lay his head anywhere he wants. He is God, after all. Jesus was saying that the cost of following him is total surrender. He says the same thing today. *"Follow me; be willing to not have even a bed or a place to lay your head."* Oh, come on, Jesus, you can't be serious. We, your followers in the western church, do not want to hear that!

Trust me, I am not a sell everything, give it all away, and diminish *all of* my resources type of guy. But, do I believe we need to ask with proper motive to receive? Absolutely, I do. Then, be wise in our stewardship? Correct. If God gives us the increase, it is for his glory, and it really has little to do with our pleasure. Let me encourage you to make wise kingdom investments. Let the return be sown back into kingdom work. Pray like it all depends on God, which it does, and work like there is no tomorrow. (Which is not guaranteed, I might add.)

Follow Jesus with all your heart. Ask Holy Spirit to lead you to all truth, to do all things to glorify the Father. Even if you do not have a soft pillow to lay your head on, your life will be satisfying knowing that you are, and always have been, part of a bigger story – a part of history, *His story*.

4:4 *"You adulterous people, don't you know that friendship with the world means enmity against God? Therefore, anyone who chooses to be a friend of the world becomes an enemy of God."*

Ok we understand that we are not to worship the world or anything in it, but can't we just be friends? I mean, after all, one of the most famous scriptures in the entire Bible, **John 3:16,** reads:

"For God so loved the world that he gave his one and only son. That whoever believes in him shall not perish, but have eternal life." So what are we to extract from James 4:4 when friendship with the world is hatred towards God?

Without getting into the Greek meanings for world – including "Kosmos", "Pantes," and others- keep in mind that this verse does not read *"Friendship with the world, and everything in it."* If we love the world more than our hope in heaven, we are all enemies of God!

74

We were never meant to be permanent residents of planet earth. Yes, God created the world and put us here, but, since the fall of mankind in the garden, this world and the world's ways should hold nothing for us.

In John 3:16, "world" could be interpreted as "pantes." This means everyone on earth – people. In *James 4:4,* "world" could be interpreted as "Kosmos." This planet earth, with its beauty and trappings, holds some men as if they were caught with no means of escaping. If you have no hope of heaven, it would be hard not to love earth. Let's put it in the following terms: *like stuff, love people.* Got it? LIKE STUFF... LOVE PEOPLE.

C.S. Lewis said in *Mere Christianity:* "*Enemy-Occupied -Territory – that is what this world is. Christianity is the story of how the **rightful king** has landed; you might say in disguise and now is calling us to take part in a great campaign of sabotage.*"

James is saying that, if we are not taking part in bringing down the enemy's strongholds, and if we are not taking part in the rescue operations of people from the world, then we are as adulterous people that has turned our collective back on our first love. We should not act like we belong here on planet earth, and for sure not live as we are just passing through.

Let's read James 4-6 from **The Message**

James 4:6

"You're cheating on God. If all you want is your own way, flirting with the world every chance you get, you end up enemies of God and his way. And do you suppose God doesn't care? The proverb has it that "he's a fiercely jealous lover." And what he gives in love is far better than anything else you'll find. It's common knowledge that "God goes against the willful proud; God gives grace to the willing humble."

Being a friend in enemy-occupied territory is similar to being a sympathizer during wartime. Yes, you see all the wrongs, but you do nothing to help rescue families from devastation, hoping that the enemy will leave you and your family alone. Well, guess what? Your enemy, the devil, wants to see you dead, broke, discouraged, and ineffective for the kingdom of God, even if you ignore him all day long.

One of the biggest lies that people have bought into is, Satan is a fairytale and that Hell is not a real place. It is curious to me that some people believe Heaven is real at the same time that they believe Hell is not. Hell is a real place, and your mortal enemy has a name. It is Satan. Our job is to be friends of God and sons and daughters of the most high. We are to advance the kingdom of light into a dark and dying world, so that people actually have a chance to go to a very real place after this life. It is called Heaven, and that place has been prepared for all followers of Christ!

Just read John 14 if you want to be encouraged and comforted by the words of Jesus:

Jesus Comforts His Disciples

John 14:1-7
"Do not let your hearts be troubled. You believe in God[a]; believe also in me. ₂ My Father's house has many rooms; if that were not so, would I have told you that I am going there to prepare a place for you? ₃ And if I go and prepare a place for you, I will come back and take you to be with me that you also may be where I am. ₄ You know the way to the place where I am going."

Jesus the Way to the Father

₅ Thomas said to him, "Lord, we don't know where you are going, so how can we know the way?" ₆ Jesus answered, "I am the way and the truth and the life. No one comes to the Father except through me. ₇ If you really know me, you will know[a] my Father as well. From now on, you do know him and have seen him."

4:5 "Or do you think Scripture says without reason that he jealously longs for the spirit he has caused to dwell in us?"

Man's spirit must be open in order to receive teaching from the Holy Spirit. Even before we were born again, before we were regenerated beings, we were spiritual. The problem was that we followed the spirit of the world. I belonged to the kingdom of darkness. Not only by choice, but by birth right! My spirit was highly developed to lie, cheat, and seek after pleasures of the flesh. I was in it only for me. Oh, the people who knew me would have said I was a nice guy. And they would have been right, or so it would have appeared, at least from the world's standards.

Here, James is making a statement that may cause us to scratch our heads and say, very intently, *"Why in the world would James say that to us?"* The answer to our question is found in our question. Why in the *world…*

If we follow the world and all of its ways, we will allow the natural, and not the godly, to control us. Our human hearts will be filled with envy, sometimes intense envy, toward others and toward the things we desire to have. How else can we explain why large groups of people in our society use class envy to accomplish a political goal?

With the condition of the human heart, we see people who have intense envy for money, power, and things, so much so that they are willing to riot in the streets to bring down the very people who have worked hard to "make it."

This envy, when joined with other people who share in this envy, becomes like the tower of Babel (see Gen 11:6). "*If as one people speaking the same language they have begun to do this, then nothing they plan to do will be impossible for them."*

This class warfare is nothing more than a group of people joined together in envy. The enemy knows how powerful this emotion is, and he uses it to bring about the strife and evil ambition we read about in James 3:14-16. Remember: *"For where you have envy and selfish ambition there you will find disorder and every evil practice."*

If allowed to prosper, this tactic will bring a once-great nation to its knees. The free nation that past generations have known will be but a distant memory. In summary, our worldly spirit is full of strife and disorder because of intense envy! The only way to have success and victory over it is to allow the Holy Spirit to reign over our natural spirit.

4:6 "But he gives us more grace. That is why Scripture says:

'God opposes the proud
but shows favor to the humble
(Proverbs 3:34).'"

God gives us more grace. Wow, think about that. *"More Grace."* More grace than we will ever need? More grace to overcome the trappings of this world? More grace than we deserve? Yes, yes, and yes! When we humble ourselves before God, trust Jesus, obey his word, and follow the Holy Spirit, grace abounds. On the other hand, when we are prideful and full of the world and ourselves, how can we expect any good thing from God? As a matter of fact, if we are driven by pride, we can expect a fall.

Read *Proverbs 16:18-19* "*Pride goes before destruction a haughty spirit before a fall. (19) Better to be lowly in spirit along with the oppressed than share plunder with the proud. So we humbly come before the Lord, knowing we can do nothing out of self, but can do all things in Christ who strengthens us. Submit yourselves, then, to God. Resist the devil, and he will flee from you.*"

4:7 "Submit yourselves, then, to God. Resist the devil, and he will flee from you."

Do we really believe that Satan will flee from us? Or have we never thought about it before? Let me share some wisdom and truth with you. The devil could care less about you. He just wants to steal, kill, and destroy. If you have trusted Jesus and made him Lord of your life, Satan sees you as his mortal enemy.

When we submit to our Father God, he builds up our spiritual strength; we then have the will and courage to resist the enemy. We are to stand up to temptation and to the ways of this world. We are to enter into this *"enemy-occupied territory"* prepared for battle.

Rarely do we hear an equipping message, as it relates to spiritual warfare, in today's church.

Spiritual warfare was once taught in the church. Over the generations, we have seen the gospel and the power of the gospel get watered down in many of the churches. Think of the early church, when the memory was fresh from having seen Jesus cast out demons, heal men of leprosy, restore sight to the blind, and raise the dead.

Yes, the early followers of Christ witnessed attacks from the enemy of God similar to the attacks we face today. But they built up one another's faith. They were told strong stories of a virgin birth and of an extremely wise and spiritually strong man, who was beaten for our iniquities and pierced for our transgressions.

This man was put to death on a cross. He is Christ, the savior, who took the sins of the world upon himself and whose blood ran down those pieces of wood. The nails in his hands and feet, the blood, the sinless blood that fell to the ground, and puddle where no more could be absorbed into the earth. There were witnesses to the warfare, when it looked like their leader was finished. They even heard him say, *"It is finished,"* while hanging from the cross! But, three days later, he came out of the tomb, victorious.

Jesus rose from the dead, showed himself to over 500 witnesses, and made certain we would know that, in him, there is victory for sure. So, here and now, in enemy-occupied territory, we can boldly claim that we were raised with Christ. We stand firm on the rock of our salvation, and Satan and all his demons must flee. They must go in the mighty name of Jesus the Christ.

Yes, we are part of the resistance movement in this battle on planet earth. We must fight each battle to secure where we stand. Then, we advance the kingdom of light. We advance God's kingdom and occupy our area with a good defense. But we must also take the fight to the enemy. Scary? Not when you know the battle has already been secured.

I want you to get this picture when you pray. You may also want to consider doing this every day.

From **Ephesians 6:10**

We put on the **helmet** of salvation
– *Lord protect our minds*
The **breastplate** of righteousness
– *Lord protect our hearts*
The **waist belt** of truth
– *Lord buckle us with your truth*
The **footwear** in preparation of the gospel
– *Lord prepare our every step*
We **gird up** our loins,
– *Lord keep us sexually pure and strong*
We then lift up our **shield of faith**
– *Lord increase our faith.*
Take our **sword** of the spirit
– *Lord we trust your mighty word*

We will not shrink back. We will run to the battle, and we will shout the victory cry. It is, in Christ, we have the ability to resist the enemy, and the enemy must flee. It is in Christ alone. The world knows little of the mighty power of God, but the church longs to see it in operation in the lives of his people.

4:8 *"Come near to God and he will come near to you. Wash your hands, you sinners, and purify your hearts, you double-minded."*

James lets us know, with no uncertain terms, that the only way we have power to overcome is when we come near to God. It is there, when we concentrate on living in his heart, that we find peace and nearness. We find that he is so very near us, that we, through his son, become a part of his story. We find him in our very breath. We find that we are given a new heart. As sinners with "unclean hands" and "double minds," we need to know we can come near to God. We need to feel like our hearts have been made pure, because of our oneness with Father!

A few years back, while driving on an interstate during the early morning hours, I heard the voice of the Lord say, *"Concentrate on living in my heart."* I looked around the car, and my wife and children were asleep. The voice seemed so very familiar, but not like theirs.

Jesus said, *"My sheep know my voice."* I kind of understand that, now. It takes such a focus to be in God's heart. I am a simple man, and I get that. When I struggle and search for answers, I have found that the best place to experience peace, to experience his presence, is right there in the heart of God. How much closer can you be? If we are one in Christ, we are one with God.

One + one + one + one does not equal four. It equals ONE.

God + Jesus + Holy Spirit + You = ONENESS

You have been invited into this great and wonderful relationship. You might as well leave the baggage of the past behind. You won't need it for this journey!

4:9 *"Grieve, mourn and wail. Change your laughter to mourning and your joy to gloom."*

4:10 *"Humble yourselves before the Lord, and he will lift you up."*

Let me get this right. We are to grieve, mourn, and wail. Quit laughing, start mourning, and let our joy become gloomy. Ok. This does not sound like my Lord. The same God who says in Proverbs 12:22: *"A cheerful heart is good medicine but a crushed spirit dries up the bones."*

Thank God that we are not left with just verse nine to ponder! It is so very true that a crushed spirit dries up the bones. Have you ever experienced that in your life? I have. When my father left us, my spirit was crushed without even knowing it. I was less than a year old. Later in life, when my family left, my heart felt like it had been broken. My crushed spirit led to the feeling that my bones were drying up. Have you felt that?

Maybe the promotion you really wanted and thought you deserved was given to someone else. Or maybe your family is grieving the loss of a loved one who was taken out of this life way to early. Maybe you just got the medical report, and the prognosis doesn't look good. Or you just found out your child was sexually abused by a neighbor.

There are so many challenges in this life. They can crush your spirit. James is telling us to grieve, mourn, and wail, but he has laid out for us a very simple process for not only surviving, but for thriving. If the focus is on you, and not on the Lord God, the simplicity will be lost.

When you die to self, there is a letting go, a mourning process. In death, we should rejoice. But it seems we have a hard time with it. Just the other day, someone said, "Rejoice in death, and be sad in birth. This world, and everything in it, is filled with pain."

While that may be true, I think we can rejoice in birth and death. Both are at the hand of the sovereign Lord God.

The death and dying process needs to be experienced in most of our lives. Not the actual physical death, but a dying to self, so that we may bury the old man once and for all. Once we do that, we can experience the resurrected life of Christ within us while we are alive and breathing here on earth.

This is the point of baptism: to bury the old man and wash away the past. The water is symbolic. We go down into the water and then rise out of it as a new creature, rejoicing and full of the spirit of God. The old man is washed away, and the new man is alive and clean. This is a very symbolic process that James speaks of. If only we, who are called by his name, would humble ourselves. Unfortunately, most people get the wrong picture of Biblical humility.

A few years ago, my wife and I visited Europe for a three week period. We toured several countries, including England, France, Holland, Austria, Germany, and others. My favorite place was Switzerland: the majestic Alps, the beauty of God's creation, the food, and the down-filled comforters. In most of our journeys, there were times when it was very humbling to be from the United States. We are such a young nation, compared to these countries that have generations of history! I remember telling someone after we returned to the states, "They have outhouses older than the USA."

Yes, I was humbled by their history, but I was no less proud to be an American. God is asking us to remain humble and to humble ourselves before him. He is so majestic that we are to humble ourselves. Then, "... he will lift us up." In other words, avoid self pride, and know that he is God. With that right position, we become so very useful in the kingdom.

We must avoid pride. We must position ourselves in Christ, humbly serve a father who loves us, and then he will lift us up. He will turn the mourning into joy. He will lift us up to do bigger, greater, and more kingdom-minded things that will bring glory to him and not to self.

4:11 *"Brothers and sisters, do not slander one another. Anyone who speaks against a brother or sister or judges them speaks against the law and judges it. When you judge the law, you are not keeping it, but sitting in judgment on it."*

Have you ever heard the expression, "Being judge and jury?" James is once again addressing an issue that was prevalent in his day – people judging people. I guess this is still around. Have you ever been judged? Rightly or wrongly, judged? Most likely, you have. I know I have. It is very unfortunate, but it seems that one of society's and the church's favorite roles is that of judge. We judge one another, gain a conviction, and then pass sentence on the other person, all in the name of justice.

All of this happens when we ourselves don't want to be judged. I am not qualified to judge the law, let alone to judge the grace of God. Are you? Many of us want so much to see our loved ones changed. We want for them the same type of change that we have experienced firsthand. Sometimes, we want this so much that we may come across as judgmental without even trying.

Let me give you an example. Let's say we ask a friend or family member if they are going to church, or if they have found a good church yet. Our heart is saying, *"I found the help I needed, the love and acceptance that has helped me over the years, in the church, and I really want that for you and your family."* That is our intent. Not to threaten, just a simple question. But some of our closest friends or family members take that question, and they hear, "Why aren't you going to church? Man, you need it. How are you ever going to measure up?"

What is the difference? I guess the lesson is to speak from our hearts in love and mercy, and not from our head in judgment. Choose your words carefully, and let everyone know that God loves them. I, for one, do not feel qualified to sit in judgment over anyone. God knows the hearts of his people. He alone is worthy to judge.

4:12 *"There is only one Lawgiver and Judge, the one who is able to save and destroy. But you—who are you to judge your neighbor?"*

The evidence is compelling and clear. On this, I rest my case, Judge.

Boasting About Tomorrow

4:13 *"Now listen, you who say, "Today or tomorrow we will go to this or that city, spend a year there, carry on business and make money."*

4:14 *"Why, you do not even know what will happen tomorrow. What is your life? You are a mist that appears for a little while and then vanishes."*

Well, that puts this life into perspective. Have you ever made big plans for you and your business, or for your family? Have you ever thought it would be great to have the million-dollar idea, make tons of money, and then do what you really want to do? Let me ask you this question: what do you really want? I mean, if money were no object, what would you be doing right now?

I would suggest that it is not the money you are looking for. When James reminds us that this life is a mist- just a vapor- and that we don't even know what will happen tomorrow, does that discourage you? Discourage you even just a little?   It does discourage most people, because many of us like to make plans. We will spend more time planning a vacation than we spend planning our lives. We love to plan, and, as long as there is tomorrow, what's the rush?

Let me have my dreams, plans, schemes, and things, and I'll take action tomorrow. A wise man once said that tomorrow never comes. That is so true, and, if tomorrow does come, who is to say that you or I will be there to greet its arrival?

There are no guarantees, but you and I are here today. Right now! Right here! So, let's settle on no discouragement for the future, but encouragement for today! We must take each moment to live. Don't ask what the world needs; ask yourself what God desires of you, because the world needs people who are alive and productive in Him today! Ask how, in this very moment in time, you can glorify the father, and then go do it. It really is that easy.

If you are breathing, there is a purpose. If your heart is beating, there is time. Choose this day to come alive for the glory of God. Why wait? You may not have tomorrow. But you have now. Trust Jesus with your life, and place it at the center of God's heart. Let the Holy Spirit lead you on- Now.

4:15 "Instead, you ought to say, 'If it is the Lord's will, we will live and do this or that.'"

4:16 "As it is, you boast in your arrogant schemes. All such boasting is evil."

4:17 "If anyone, then, knows the good they ought to do and doesn't do it, it is sin for them."

If we are wise, we must realize that we are not in control. We can plan, set goals, dream, and pray for many things. However, if we leave out the most important person (the Lord), or the most important aspect of our plans (the Lord's will), then this life can be unspiritual, unsettling, and unfulfilling.

Jesus said, *"And when you pray..."* (He didn't say "if" you pray...) *He said to pray, "Your kingdom come, your will be done."* It was not to create a rhyme. He was showing us that even the Son of God prays, *"If it is the Lord's will..."* Verse 16, hits the nail on the head. You boast and brag. All such boasting is evil.

Have you ever been around someone who has to let you know what kind of car they drive, the place they live, or how much money they have made? As to make themselves appear important? I have, and it makes that person look so shallow, so bad. They are trying to impress you with such talk.

Being braggadocios and putting on airs seems phony, doesn't it? I, for one, think it does. Then, there are the "name droppers?" Oh yeah? We are supposed to be impressed that you know so and so, and that they have a big mansion, and wrote that book? You know the people I am talking about.

I have done this myself. I used to, in my seminars, drop the fact that I have had lunch with US Presidents, traveled the globe, met leaders, and had Christmas dinner with Heisman Trophy winners. Yes, I have been guilty of that. But now, I think, "So what?" How does that advance the kingdom of God? I am grateful for the people I have met and the places I have been, but nothing compares to the King I met many years ago. His name is Jesus.

This King? Oh yeah, we still keep in touch. As a matter of fact we talk most days. Even though he is the king of kings, hanging out with him is like hanging out with a good friend, or a guy that's closer than a brother. Hey, you want to know something else? He told me to tell you, "Hello." If you have never met him, he really wants to get to know you! Oh yeah, I can introduce you two. Seriously, just let me know. My contact info is on the back of this book.

But just so there is no misunderstanding- the boasting and the bragging is not a good thing. As a matter of fact, our friend James calls it evil. He then drops this bomb: *anyone* (I think that's us) *who knows the good he ought to do, and doesn't do it, sins.*

 Come on, James! You didn't have to throw that in, did you? But I guess that makes sense. When we study scripture, we begin to realize that, as a follower of Christ, we are now presented with a new reality. First, we are not alone; we are his. We are now part of a new family- the family of God.

We are connected in the spirit at the heart level, with millions of brothers and sisters around the world. Think of that! You will never be alone again. And, as in any family, there are opportunities to succeed and to fail. But we can no longer sit back and expect someone else to do all that needs to be done. We cannot do all of it, but we can do something.

We must realize that the Lord has placed in us certain gifts and talents. He has placed them there so that we may develop and use them for kingdom work. Keep in mind that everything we do should glorify God the father. If I work at an auto repair shop, a coffee shop, or an ice cream shop, how I act, my quality of work, and the way I treat people, should reflect the love, grace, and mercy that he has poured into me. I have been filled up to give out.

As we study the Word, the good we should do becomes apparent. It is not just written on the pages of the Bible; it is written on our hearts. Jesus, in the beatitudes (Matthew 5), lays it out with words like "meek," "mercy," "heart," "peace," "righteousness," and "kingdom of heaven."

This needs to be our posture as we walk through our brief journey on planet earth. We ought to pray, not worry, walk by faith, and not judge others. We need to get the plank out of our own eye *(Matt 7);* so that we can see clearly what the Lord would have us do. Then, we should actually do it. We go for it! We do it, and, in doing so, we avoid all kinds of sin. I hope that makes sense.

Take a few minutes to reflect. What is the Heavenly Father speaking to your heart? Is there something that you know you should do? Listen close, and then obey.

Warning to Rich Oppressors

5:1 *"Now listen, you rich people, weep and wail, because of the misery that is coming upon you."*

We read that and think, "Whew, I'm glad I am not rich! Those people will be miserable." Let me ask you and I a question. By the standards of the world, are you and I not rich? Do we not have more than 90 percent of the world's population?

Sometimes we possess so much that it is considered excessive by most of the world. Well, I am not rich. Really? Do you want to go there? I grew up in a home where my mom worked to put food on the table, gas in the car, and the lights on at the little house where she and six kids called home. I remember that Fridays were my favorite day. She stopped at the grocery store on the way home from work, and she filled the back seat with bags of canned goods, gallons of milk, and dozens of eggs. Even when things were tight, she would try and get treats for us kids- Twinkies, or Little Debbie snacks.

One time, she even joined a record club and let us kids pick a record album to ship right to our door.

Those albums became prized possessions, to all us kids; because they were something we could call our own! I am going to risk dating myself to share this with you. I remember one time, I picked a *Loving Spoonful* album, and, when it arrived, I almost wore that thing out! *"Do you believe in Magic"* and *"Summer in the City"* became my favorite songs that summer.

Another time, my brother picked a Beatles album, and when it arrived we realized he had picked *"Kate Smith, sings The Beatles."* (Check out **Kathryn Elizabeth "Kate" Smith** on Wikipedia). What a disaster!

We heated with a woodstove in that house. We got 2 or 3 channels on our old black and white Sears TV. My older brother and I shared a little room that had been added to the house, and there were times that the snow actually blew through the cracks in the walls and covered our blankets. That is one story my kids found hard to believe! We had two pairs of pants and two shirts for the school week. We worked all summer to buy them. We picked tomatoes, strawberries, or anything else we could to earn our "school clothes" money.

Were we poor? I guess, by America's standards, we would have been in that category. But compared to the rest of the world, we had food, a car, clothes, a house, and a record player for listening to *Kate Smith singing Hey Jude*. Heck, we were rich!

So, when James says, "Listen, you rich people," I think we qualify. There is a word for all in these passages.

5:2 *"Your wealth has rotted and moths have eaten your clothes."*

5:3 *"Your gold and silver are corroded. Their corrosion will testify against you and eat your flesh like fire. You have hoarded wealth in the last days."*

It really is about perspective. When we say "rich" or "wealthy," most of us think about someone else. But, had you been born in parts of India, or left as orphan in Romania or Africa, your perspective would be very different. If an American shows up on a mission trip, you might think that this American must be rich. After all, they are from the richest nation on earth.

And why wouldn't you think that? Our nation, America, has done so much humanitarian good around the world, in war-torn regions and in the slums and dumps where children scavenge for food or trinkets to sell in order to survive.

Yet, there are people here in this great country that want to tear down the rich, punish them for success, and, in the name of "fairness," confiscate their wealth and redistribute that wealth to others.

This Robin Hood mentality goes against what has made America great. America, at one time, was the land of opportunity. Oh, of course, there are some wealthy people who have never helped another person. While this is unfortunate, it still is not a crime to be rich.

Now it seems that, if you earn it, the government will take it and waste it. Oh, what a country we have become- where a rich county like ours takes prayer out of the schools, makes patriotism a bad thing, and sees Christians who live out biblical faith as kooks.

I guess we should weep and wail. The concept of "work hard to earn a better future for your family" is almost a thing of the past. Greed and class warfare have taken its place. To some people living in the greatest country on earth, the federal government has taken the place of God, and the social programs have replaced the local church.

Wealth. Yes, it is rotten. Moths have eaten our clothes, while gold and silver have taken us away from compassion and mercy. Hoarding wealth or keeping up with our ever-shrinking 401K's have given us reasons to weep and wail. But the truly tragic aspect of all this is that the focus is so much on self. Focused on self, we miss wonderful opportunities to help those in need.

During the holidays, we are confronted with giving choices all the time. Think about it, as Americans, we flock to the stores and malls with our physical wealth to exchange it for wrapped trinkets to give loved ones under the tree. Do we love to give, or are we expected to do even more than last year?

Think about giving. We walk into many of these shopping malls and stores during this special time of faith, friends, and family. We hear bells ringing to get our attention. Once we see the red kettle, we remember, "Oh yeah, there are people who are actually worse off than I am."

I am compelled to give. If I have no cash, I feel a little tinge of guilt. Am I the only one? But, when we drop some change, or a few bucks, into that kettle and hear, "Merry Christmas," it feels like we actually made a difference. In a small way, we have.

What if we could feel that every day? The needs of the hurting do not go away the other 11 months of the year. Again, we can't do it all, but we can do something. Our wealth will not corrode, or testify against us, if we seek wisdom and direction to give where God directs.

The poor will always be among us – and hopefully the rich will be, too. The rich people who get it, that is, and understand how to use that wealth for kingdom good. If not, we can continue to hoard, to worry, and to watch the riches of this fallen. Jesus said, *"So, when you give to the needy."* Not "if" you give to the needy, but "when" you give.

He also teaches us a Godly perspective of treasure. *"Do not store up for yourself treasures on earth where moth and rush destroy."* Sound familiar? *These riches will testify against you and eat your flesh like fire."* Man, that is a little harsh, don't you think? Sometimes, the truth hurts.

5:4 *"Look! The wages you failed to pay the workman who mowed your fields are crying out against you. The cries of the harvesters have reached the ears of the Lord Almighty."*

This passage speaks of fairness. When we have a job to be done, we normally have identified, up front, what the payment will be. When we agree to do a job, the same principal holds true. Do it well, and make sure the employer gets their money's worth.

When Jesus was sending out the 72 (see Luke 10:2), he made it a point to give them instructions. He said, *".....a worker deserves his wages."* So, as we read here in James, we must realize that there are opportunities to do the right thing. We need to make sure we just do it!

James is speaking to the rich oppressors. How can this apply to us? We try to be fair in business, of course. We try to negotiate the best deal by saying, "That's just good business," but the goal of a Christ follower is that all parties be satisfied at the end of the transaction.

Let me ask you this question: have you ever bragged about the "deal" you made? I have met people like that- people who find glee in getting the best of someone else. They believe they are shrewd in business. I think I would rather be remembered as fair in business.

5:5 "You have lived on earth in luxury and self-indulgence. You have fattened yourselves in the day of slaughter."

5:6"You have condemned and murdered innocent men who were not opposing you."

When James speaks of living on earth in luxury and self-indulgence, I go back again to our high standard of living compared to the rest of the world. The key for us believers is to not be oppressive in our wealth. And when James says, "You have fattened yourselves in the day of slaughter," I think, "*I could drop a few pounds, and I need to exercise more, but what is this 'day of slaughter' stuff?*"

James gives us some insight into mankind. If a person sins against his own body, it normally is considered stupidity. An example of this would be for someone to smoke, drink too much, or eat too much. This behavior is self-indulging, is a waste of money, and is a waist that is ever-expanding. This over-indulgence is not just wasteful; it shows a lack of self-discipline.

Just because we can, doesn't mean we should. When I was a teenager, through a series of unfortunate events I ended up with a place of my own. I had a little 3-bedroomhouse on the edge of town. Of course, without adult supervision, it became the party place for my friends from high school. "Friday night at Mel's place" became the battle cry during the week at school. I knew right from wrong, and I knew I could still get in trouble, so rarely did I have big parties. But I did have a bunch of small ones.

Just because I could have a party every weekend didn't mean that I should. I did indulge my flesh, and I did some pretty stupid things, but I thank God for seeing me through it. I survived. I could have destroyed myself, but God had other plans.

When we read "the day of slaughter," there are several things that come to mind. One is a common occurrence. Before we had supermarkets with all the products lined up on the shelves neat and tidy, and before there were dairy cases and meat cases organized with expiration dates right there on the label, families used to pick one lucky cow, or pig, in the spring. They would set aside this animal so that it could be fed a special diet of grains. This "fattening up" process would normally last several months, or as long as a year.

Once the animal was fat and happy, due to the special treatment, the family would schedule a day of slaughter for this animal. Most of the family would be included.

When the work started, everyone had a role, and every part of the animal was used to supply the family with what was needed for the year. A good skinner can down a beef and have it loaded in the truck, headed to the meat locker plant, in less than 30 minutes. After months of fattening, the day of slaughter comes.

We live excessively in America. It is as if we are on a special diet of grains. We get fat and happy. In the land of plenty, we eat more than plenty. Instead of knowing when to say "When," we fatten ourselves. We over-indulge our senses and our lifestyles, and the day of slaughter comes. The day of reckoning cannot be avoided. If we over-indulge our fleshly desires and actually think that there will be no consequences, we had best think again.

We have condemned and murdered innocent men who were not opposing us? Whoa. Hold on, James! I have never murdered anyone! I am fairly certain that I have not condemned anyone with my words or killed anyone with my thoughts. For sure, I have not killed anyone physically!

Since these words were written, mankind has found new ways to condemn whole people groups. Evil men who gained riches and power have used both to perform ungodly acts- even devilish acts- against people for no reason.

Think of it. The Romans crucified Christians, or threw them in pits with hungry lions; Hitler wanted to exterminate all Jews from the face of the earth. During the Holocaust, it is generally thought that Hitler was responsible for the deaths of 6 million Jewish people.

Talk about having condemned and murdered innocent men, women, and children who were not opposing him! This is just one human tragedy in recorded history. It should wake us up to the fact that humans can do such things to other humans.

In America, we will condemn and destroy the lives of 3,304 innocent children, daily! That's 23,196 every week, 100,516 every month, and 1,206,192 every year! Did you catch that? One million, two hundred six thousand, one hundred ninety two, per year! Roe vs. Wade was passed in 1973. At this writing, that would mean close to 55,000,000 million kids dead, in the US alone. Since 1980, that number worldwide is 1,240,134,430. Over one billion lives were never given a chance. They were condemned and murdered. James had it right. Without a moral compass, a society can place no value on life.

Human beings will do horrible things in the name of convenience and self interest. The cries of injustice have reached the ears of the Lord Almighty, and I guess the message for all of us is to repent, trust God, and follow his righteous ways. James communicates to us, *"Submit yourselves then to God, resist the devil, he will flee. Come near to God, and he will come near to you."*

We say, "YES," to Lord Jesus! We say, "NO," to Satan. He is a liar, and the father of lies!

Patience in Suffering

5:7 "Be patient, then, brothers and sisters, until the Lord's coming. See how the farmer waits for the land to yield its valuable crop, patiently waiting for the autumn and spring rains."

Have you ever had a garden? How about a farm? We had a garden when the kids were small. Getting the soil ready, choosing what to plant- that was all a family affair. Once the seeds were in the ground, we worked while we waited. Weeding the garden, watering daily, and the excitement of a garden can wear off quickly when nothing is out of the ground.

We explained to the kids that we must be patient, that the seed was there, and that we had to trust that it was going to grow. But we had to work while we waited. Then, one day, something would break the top soil. The evidence of the plowing and tilling of the soil, the planting of the seed, the watering, and the weeding would all be confirmed in that little plant. It was usually a bean plant, because they grow the fastest.

Just like our faith, the kids were renewed when they saw that the corn, carrots, lettuce, and okra would follow. It was a great lesson in patience.

5:8 *"You too be patient and stand firm because the Lords coming is near."*

When a seed is placed in the ground, it dies. It dies so that the new life that was trapped inside might grow out of it. We, in the same way, must take our seed (the deposit of faith) and die to ourselves, so that faith in Christ may grow in our hearts and produce a crop of righteousness. As with the farmer, we patiently prepare our hearts. We plant the seed of faith, and then we work while we wait!

James says, *"The Lord's coming is near."* Does that mean anything to you? People, for generations, have thought the return of Christ could happen in their lifetime. And it could. I have often wondered about the second coming of Christ. We are told the day and the hour are not known to men. That's good enough for me. But we are to watch and be ready, to not be surprised by current events. He is coming back!

I have a question for you. Christ came as a baby to planet earth. He came into my and your heart when we were saved. He is coming back to earth. As a believer in Christ, will this be the second or the third coming of Jesus? Think about it. The main point is, we are to be patient. We are to stand firm on our faith, and, in doing so, we stand together as believers. We plant, and we work while we wait. The harvest is ready.

5:9 *"Don't grumble against each other, brothers and sisters, or you will be judged. The judge is standing by the door!"*

Again, James reminds us to remember that our judge- good, faithful, true, and certain- stands ever ready. When we grumble against each other, we go against the golden rule, which, by the way, used to be taught in our homes and schools. *"Do unto others, as you have them do unto you." "Treat others the way you want to be treated."*

We have taken this really good thing and made it, once again, about us! Have you ever heard, "Do it to others before they do it to you?" When we grumble, complain, or speak poison, we will be judged. Maybe we need to get this picture. Jesus is with us, in us, and we move and live and have our being in him.

So, in every step and every action, he is with you. He is there, at the door, so we need to act like it. Our peace when we stand in the face of adversity might be how the world sees Christ. Our words and our grumbling are hopefully not how they know we are his.

5:10 "Brothers and sisters, as an example of patience in the face of suffering, take the prophets who spoke in the name of the Lord."

5:11 "As you know, we count as blessed those who have persevered. You have heard of Job's perseverance and have seen what the Lord finally brought about. The Lord is full of compassion and mercy."

James is showing us, by example, those who had suffered. The prophets suffered. They had to be so patient throughout the ages. These men had a call of God on their lives, to deliver hard news and to go forward.

Theirs was news that, most of the time, made someone mad. It even put their life at risk. But they spoke with authority in the name of the Lord. Today, we shrink back from speaking the truth, because we are living in a time when things are so politically correct that we dare not speak truth. We don't want to offend someone. Someone will not like us on Facebook. I have a question: is backbone out of style and linguine spine in style?

Of course, we are to speak the truth in love. Christ is our example; all through the New Testament, he was speaking the truth. So was John the Baptist, when he was put in prison. What follows is nothing more than God's divine provision for Jesus.

Jesus spent 40 days in the desert in the wind, hungry, thirsty, and went face-to-face with Satan. Tempted by the evil one, he stood up to the temptations, using scripture to fight back. Filled with the spirit, he walks out of the wilderness!

Let's pick up the story in Mark 1:14. *"After John was put into prison Jesus went into Galilee proclaiming the good news of God. (15) 'The time has come,' he said. 'The Kingdom of God is near. Repent and believe the good news.'*

Can you imagine if you or I were to use these very same words today? We would be radical Christians using judgmental speech. It sure would not be PC.

We can say things like, "Have you heard the good news of Christ," or, "If you will believe in Jesus, life will make sense." But if you are bold in your faith and say, "The Kingdom of God is near, so repent from your sins," the majority of people, including the religious folks, would not want to hear that. Of course, if you talk about the love and grace of God, that is a lot more acceptable.

I would be the first to say that the love, grace, and mercy that Christ has shown me have changed the course of my life. The truth is that I was hell-bound, and Jesus accepted me with arms wide open.

Love and knowing I could speak repentance over my own heart. That was the truth I had been missing. See, I now know I am a sinner saved by grace. At that time, I needed to change my life. All the self-help books and positive thinking could not hold a candle to saying "YES" to Jesus Christ. God said it, I believe it, and it is good enough for me. How about you? You are the only one who can answer that.

Today, most people think Christians are a weak bunch of people who have some good ideas. But maybe they rarely see us live them out in our own lives. To some, we are a joke. No, seriously. To prove this, all you have to do is listen to some of the great intellectual minds, or to Comedy Central. Take

108

your pick. The truth is that in this PC police state, when someone stands up for Christ or lives their faith out loud (like a Tim Tebow), the world will do everything possible to tear them down.

When Tim Tebow came out of college and joined the NFL, all it took was a couple of statements, and he was suddenly a polarizing figure who was too controversial for even Christian leaders. The controversy that arose? Well, you see- he wasn't actually afraid to speak and live what he believes.

Even some people in the church had a problem with that. Where have we gone, church? How far are we from the early church of Acts? Today, when someone who has a strong faith and takes a stand for that faith, they are nothing more than a freakish individual called; one of those, you know, a *"Christian."*

Think of persecution, patience, and suffering? These words are for biblical characters or for people around the world living under the vale or dictators, socialism, or communism, right? Look around, my friend. The kingdom of heaven is near. Will you speak the truth- the good news- no matter what the cost?

James tells us, *"We consider blessed those who have been persecuted."* Blessed? Then, he uses Job as an example. Have you ever heard someone say, "Oh, I am as blessed as Job?" Probably hadn't heard that one lately. Most people, when they compare themselves to Job, reference some suffering they are going through. As an example of perseverance, we are given the book of Job in the Old Testament. We are told Job was blameless and upright. He feared God and shunned evil.

Job was well-off, and he owned sheep, camels, oxen, donkeys, and had a great number of servants. "He was the greatest man among the people of the east," the Bible says. He was a family man with three daughters and seven sons.

God's increase and a hedge of protection was around him, but, for some reason, God allowed Satan to hold everything Job had in his hands. Read the story in Job. Father God was pleased with Job. After all, he said, *"There is none on earth like him."* But God allowed Satan to take everything Job had in his hands! In one day, Job lost his sheep, camels, oxen, donkeys, and servants. All were captured, killed, or burned– everything.

Also on that day, Job lost his sons and daughters. Do you think he was persecuted? Yes, in the worst way. But, in all this trouble, Job did not sin by blaming God. Read it. He was then afflicted with painful sores from the soles of his feet to the top of his head. His wife then made an interesting statement: *"Curse God, and die!"*

He could have responded with something like, *"Well, thank you very much, my dear sweet wife. You go first, I dare you."* Now, admit it. We might have said something like that, but Job did not. He said, *"You are talking like a foolish woman."* Then he made a statement we can all benefit from. Job continued, *"Shall we accept good from God, and not trouble?"* There is the crux of the matter. Satan wants us to deny or curse God when things do not go our way, when we seemingly lose our stuff.

We expect things should be "rosy," because we are believers and followers of Christ. But let's not forget- we are living in a fallen world. Yes, we rejoice in the blessings of God, but do we rejoice only when things are going well?

As followers of Christ, we need to hear his words. We need to hear the words of our savior, all of them. Look at John 16:33: *"I have told you these things so that you may have peace. In this world you will have trouble. But take heart! I have overcome the world."*

Do you see that? In this fallen world, as we occupy enemy territory, we will have trouble. "You will" have trouble, so do not be surprised when it comes.

In Job's case, through his pain, sorrow, and trouble, he never cursed God or lost all faith. As a matter of fact, there is a statement in Job: *"The spirit of God has made me; the breath of the Almighty gives me life."*

What happened at the end of his life, as Job prayed for his foolish friends? Job's prayer was accepted by the Lord, and, afterward, the Lord made Job prosperous again. He gave him twice as much as he had before. The Lord blessed the latter part of his life more than the first.

111

Job lived a hundred and forty years, and he saw his children (he was given a new family) and their children to the fourth generation. He died old and full of years. Read it. In his trouble, he held on to God's sovereignty and God's will alone. In our trouble (remember, Jesus said we would have trouble), we must hang on to this next statement: *"Take heart, I have overcome the world."*

Here is the picture for us: trouble will come. God will allow trouble for our growth, even if we lose everything we have. We must depend on him alone through the pain, the suffering, the loss, and the restoration. God is God. Jesus said he has overcome the world. In Christ we, too, are overcomers.

In John, Jesus says some interesting and powerful things: *"Because I live, you will also live. I am in the Father and you are in me, and I am in you. Peace I leave with you, my peace I give you: I do not give as the world gives. Do not let your hearts be troubled, and do not be afraid."*

James wants us to know that the Lord is full of compassion and mercy. Yes, there will be trouble in this world. We will have trouble, but our hearts need not be troubled. We are one in Christ. His mercy and grace will flow to us and through us as we trust him.

God will allow trouble to grow us deeper.

5:12 "Above all, my brothers and sisters, do not swear – not by heaven or by earth or by anything else. All you need to say is a simple 'Yes' or 'No.' Otherwise you will be condemned."

How many people do you know who try to manipulate their way through life? You're not sure that "yes" means yes with them. I have found these people hard to deal with. Can people change their minds? Sure. But what is it that James wants us to understand here?

Throughout history, men have taken oaths of office. "Swearing in," we call it. Historically, in America, the person taking the oath of office raises one hand- the right hand- and places their left hand on the Holy Bible.

Before we give testimony, we repeat, *"To solemnly tell the truth, nothing but the truth so help me God."* Or, when taking the oath of office for the Presidency of the United States of America: "*I do solemnly swear that I will faithfully execute the office of President of the United States and to the best of my ability, preserve, protect, and defend the constitution of the United States."*

Recently, we have witnessed politicians who, under oath, swear to tell the truth, but then try to lie their ways out of compromising situations. We have seen church leaders fall from grace, caught in scandal. James is repeating the words that Jesus spoke in the sermon on the mount (Matthew 5:34-37): *"But I tell you, Do not swear at all, either by*

113

*heaven, for it is God's throne, or by earth, for it is
his footstool or by Jerusalem for it is the city of the
great king. And do not swear by your head, for you
cannot make even one hair white or black. Simply
let your yes be yes, and your no, no; anything
beyond this comes from the evil one."*

What we are to take away from this passage: stop
operating in the gray areas of life. Stand up, let
your "yes" be an honest answer, and let your "no"
be a truthful no. When challenges come in every
area of life, it is good to have already determined
where you stand. Your "YES" to Jesus and your
"NO" to Satan go a long way to help you walk in
integrity.

The Prayer of Faith

**5:13 *"Is anyone among you in trouble? Let
them pray. Is anyone happy? Let him sing
songs of praise."***

Here is another way to handle trouble when it
comes. We must handle it with prayer. I am sorry.
Did you just say prayer? But I pray about everything
all the time. Really, I do. Ok, that's sounds good. As
you know, there have been books and books
written on prayer and praying. There are books on
how to talk to God, or how to hear from God. I saw
a book once called, **"Shut-Up and Listen:** *the truth
about how to communicate at work."* Hum- maybe
we hear from God at work and everywhere else.

James gives us what seems to be such a natural response to when we are in trouble: PRAY! It is good to be reminded that you and I, followers of Christ, have been given such grace and mercy. There is always some appropriate response.

Trouble comes, and we pray. Feeling happy, we praise. There is always an action to be taken. Our goal should be to have godly action. That's why most of my praise is spoken, not sung. I know that some of you have beautiful voices and can sing praises to God with angelic tones. Me? Well, not so much. But I read somewhere, "Make a joyful noise unto the Lord," so that I can do.

Let's review: Happy-Praise. Trouble-Pray, or Happy-Pray, Trouble-Praise I think we got it! Now, my guess is that we will get a chance to practice both this week.

5:14 "Is anyone among you sick? Let them call the elders of the church to pray over them and anoint them with oil in the name of the Lord."

5:15 "And the prayer offered in faith will make the sick person well; the Lord will raise them up. If they have sinned, they will be forgiven."

Many of us Christians struggle with these two verses. One vain interpretation is: if you're sick, get to church, go to the front, and join your faith with the elders, have enough faith. You might be made well.

James is talking about prayer, remember? Is it the prayer that heals? Is it someone else's prayer that heals? Is it the anointing oil, in the name of the Lord, that heals?

Well, I think we may be getting closer to figuring this out. I have seen the prayers of a church produce great healing. Normally, it is in the hearts of the people. When James tells us to "call the elders or the church," we must remember that, in the early church, there were several meeting places in the community.

Acts 2:46

"Every day they continued to meet together in the temple courts. They broke bread in their homes and are together with glad and sincere hearts."

They met in the temple courts and in homes. So, if someone was sick and called upon the elders or the church to pray over them, chances are that they would actually be standing over them. See the picture? I think that we, in the western church, have made almost everything in the church routine and religious. If we could just get a glimpse of the power of simplicity, we may be able to recognize what man has done. For control and convenience, man has added layers of rules and regulations to what God has done through the saving blood of Christ.

Our healing is not some formula that man has put into place. Our faith in the Healer is well-placed, but our faith cannot heal us. The faith of a few good friends, or the faith of the elders, cannot heal us. While all of these help bring us to a place where we can receive healing, it is the Lord alone that can heal. It is the Sovereign God- Jehovah- that heals us. He alone judges, heals, and completes us in Christ Jesus.

The prayer offered by faith is strong. "If I believe, I can move God on my behalf." But the maker of the universe has sovereign reign over it all. So, when James gives us a process- *"call the elders"*- we should listen to that instruction, anoint with oil, and pray. Yes, trust God and pray that His will be done.

Too many people over the years have felt that, if they did not get total and complete healing in a matter of minutes, something was wrong with their faith. This, once again, puts the power and responsibility on the individual and not on the Lord. But Jesus said to cast our burdens on him, to trust him, and to not lean on our own understanding. Yes, he did.

It is not super faith that will heal you. Only God can. It is not the elders that will raise the sick. Only God can. It is not the oil poured over your head that will heal you. Only God can. If you have sinned, and we all have, none of these processes will forgive you. Only God will.

Putting our faith into action is a great thing. Linking our faith with other believers is also a great thing. But when we see a Sovereign God love us, heal us, and raise us up, it becomes all about him and not about us or other men.

Does that make sense? Can God heal us in an instant? Of course he can. I have seen it. Can he allow us to go through sickness before total healing, in order to grow us deeper, closer, and more dependent on him? Absolutely, I have seen that also.

For James, and I and You, we must pray and trust God, from whom all blessings flow. Praise to his holy name in our trouble and affliction. Praise him in our healing, our pain, and our forgiveness, and in it all praise Father, Son and Holy Spirit.

5:16 "Therefore confess your sins to each other and pray for each other so that you may be healed. The prayer of a righteous person is powerful and effective."

Ok. Calling on the elders of the church when I am sick is one thing, but confessing my sins to someone else? That's another story. What about that sin? You know. The one we could never confess. That sin is for God's ears only. I could not confess that to anyone but the Lord God!

Over the centuries, people have turned confession into a process where you are to show up, spill your thoughts or what you have done, repent, and say some prayers as a way of absolving sins. Brothers and sisters, I am for anything that draws us closer to God. If this process and ritual helps you, I say go for it. But do not stop there.

Saying, "I am sorry, please forgive me," is good, but repentance must take place at the heart level. It cannot just be with our lips. Father God is so loving and so faithful to forgive us. Of course, like any good father, he would prefer our obedience to our repentance.

James shares with us another truth. He is telling us that it is about the prayer. Look at it this way, while men search and search for a better process, God is searching for better men. And wouldn't you agree that he makes us better men!

He says, *"The prayer of a righteous man is powerful and effective."* I don't know about you, but I don't feel so righteous most of the time. The meaning of "righteous" needs to be understood better if we are to know if our prayers will be powerful and effective.

First, we must be right-living men. How can we believe that our prayers will be heard, if they are but words repeated from a page that someone else wrote for others? Again, if this helps you, start there. But also grow deeper in a relationship with God.

When we are in Christ- and, of course that is our only hope for true righteousness; the Father wants to hear our cries from a heart level. In that right-living our heart-level prayer becomes powerful.

Oh, we can pray from a cold heart. I guess we must start somewhere. But our prayers only become effective when spoken from a righteous life. A righteous life can only be lived in Christ. Christ does what the Father wills.

119

So, when you pray the Lord's Prayer, listen to the words. Pray them from a repentance-filled, healed heart, knowing that his grace and mercy allow us access to the Lord. Here are those words:

I have devoted a full page of this book to this prayer, in case you want to copy it and put it on your bulletin board!

**Our Father, which art in heaven,
Hallowed be thy Name.
Thy Kingdom come.
Thy will be done in earth,
As it is in heaven.
Give us this day our daily bread.
And forgive us our trespasses,
As we forgive them that trespass
against us.
And lead us not into temptation,
But deliver us from evil.
For thine is the kingdom,
The power, and the glory,
For ever and ever.
Amen.**

(Taken from the Anglican Book of Common Prayer- 1662)

Pray this prayer out loud, and listen to the powerful words you are saying and praying.

A "righteous" man also has a reverence for the one true Living God. Prayer is not flippant, or so casual that it appears comical. Yes, communication with God should be as easy as our next breath, but remember that the God we are communicating with actually gives you that next breath.

The fear and reverence of God is shown in righteous men. God wants to hear from you today. He wants all the questions, all the pain, and all the joy, no matter what you're feeling. Our Father wants all of it, and, if we want to experience effective prayer, we must give him all we are and all we are not!

He can take the unrighteous and create something of honor through Christ, his son. He can create in us his righteousness- his rightness for our wrongness. Sounds like a great trade to me!

The idea is to pray like you mean it. Pray like it must be answered, from a right heart and right motives. We must trust God to "avail much." Many times, we say our short quick prayers so that our ears hear it, making us feel better. But the next time you are faced with circumstance much bigger than you could imagine, pray from a righteous heart to a righteous God for a righteous answer. Pray it through, and do not stop! Let it be powerful and effective, due to Christ in you, the hope of glory.

5:17 "Elijah was a human being, even as we are. He prayed earnestly that it would not rain, and it did not rain on the land for three and a half year."

5:18 "Again he prayed, and the heavens gave rain, and the earth produced its crops."

James is telling us to look at Elijah, a man just like you and I. Sometimes, we take people from the Bible and turn them into superheroes. But the fact is that most were just ordinary men and women who made a decision to follow God. Then, they stuck to their decision!

When we read or hear of the great leaders of the Church- Martin Luther, Charles Spurgeon, Billy Graham – we want to put them on spiritual pedestals. Yes, these men have done great and mighty works for God. They are only men.

C.S. Lewis said, *"We meet no ordinary people in our lives."* But that may be the issue at hand. We are but ordinary men doing extraordinary things for God.

We read of extraordinary events and people, and the voice of the accuser says, "That can never be you. You have made too many mistakes, you have failed too much, and you are just a human – no wonder you have done so little with your life!" Oh, but there is Elijah- a man like us.

Just as Elijah was called as a prophet of God, you and I are called. He was obedient to do the will of God. Are you and I so focused on the mission to do the will of God that nothing else matters? Is it this factor, the "God" factor, which separates ordinary men from the heroes of our faith? I think it is.

When there is the obedience of a God-fearing man, when nothing matters as much as doing the will of the Father, prayers are answered. Prayers for no rain, prayers for rain, prayers for direction, for clarity, for opportunity, for business and for family, for this life here, and to prepare us for the next phase of eternity called heaven.

"But he was a prophet!" we say. Yes, that was his calling, and he carried it out well. In Ephesians 4:11, we read, "*It was he (Christ) who gave some to be apostles, some to be prophets, some to be evangelist, and some to be pastors and teachers.*" *This is* referred to as the fivefold ministry, and it is to prepare God's people (that's us) for works of service.

Now we're back to "faith without works is dead!" Look closely at your calling and your purpose, and you will find that God has a plan for you. Oh yes, we ordinary men. We are called to obedience and to live out our faith for the creator, Father God.

Elijah was obedient, and the rain was stopped. Elijah was obedient, the rain came, and crops were produced. A harvest of faith was produced. So, what are you and I praying for? Remember: big prayers to God will produce a big harvest for God.

We are men, just as Elijah was a man. He lived in the 9th century BC, during the years of King Ahab and Queen Jezebel. He was a man who stood against the might of kings and false prophets. We are men living in the twenty-first century AD, during a time of corrupt governments and false religions.

Elijah stood firm against the prophets. Are we standing firm against any false doctrine of the church and against the works of darkness brought on by the enemy of the ages, the enemy of God? Look around. What the world needs, and the church needs, is a people who are willing to stand. Elijah was a man just like us, and he prayed! Can we see the pattern of God at work? We must!

5:19 "To brothers and sisters, if one of you should wander from the truth and someone should bring that person back,

5:20 remember this: Whoever turns a sinner from the error of their way will save them from death and cover over a multitude of sins."

It is interesting the way James ends this conversation – abruptly, but very specific. It's almost like he is saying, *"Oh, by the way, if any of you wander from the truth- please, someone, go get him, and bring him back."*

The truth – that's what we want. To wander away is not good. It almost sounds like we are out on a walk. Because of distractions, or because we are not giving our full attention, we wander off the trail. If you walk with God, as a brother in Christ, there is a path that you need to follow.

Matthew 7:13-14

13 "Enter through the narrow gate. For wide is the gate and broad is the road that leads to destruction, and many enter through it. 14 But small is the gate and narrow the road that leads to life, and only a few find it."

We can see that there is a gate and a narrow road that lead to life. If we are not focused, or if we start our journey on the wide road followed by many, the chances are that we are headed to destruction.

Think about it. Taking the easy road most often turns out not so easy. I was the son of a mom who despised lying. In my early years, I tried to lie my way out of trouble. I actually thought it was easy, until the truth and the belt, or switch, came out! They taught me it was neither easy nor prudent.

The easy, wide road leads to destruction. But the small gate, to the narrow road, leads to life. "The gate" to life is Jesus Christ, and he is teaching us that there are two roads. We have free will to choose which road we will travel. One leads to death and hell, and the other leads to eternal life and heaven. Knowing that, why would we not choose the narrow over the broad?

It seems easy, because we have been conditioned to take that easy road. As it turns out, the road is not so easy. There really are two gates, two ways, and two destinations. Choose wisely; your very life depends on it!

At my high school graduation- back when Lassie was just a pup- we had gentleman deliver the commencement address. While I do not remember his name, all these years later I do still remember his message.

He spoke of two roads in life. He said, "There *are two roads that you can take. There is a low road or a high road."* He challenged the entire graduating class to take the high road. That road may be harder to travel at first, but it will lead to the best things in life. But the low road, the wide road traveled most, leads to heartache, disappointment, and disaster. It was wisdom that we all needed at that age. I have thought about researching where all my classmates ended up. It would be interesting to see which road we all have traveled.

When James says, "... *If one of you should wander from the truth,"* he is assuming we have found the truth. Remember that once you and I have that personal relationship with Christ, Satan wants nothing more than to kill, steal, and destroy that relationship. Think of it this way: we had a personal relationship with the world, and with all the world's ways, but then we found truth. He was always there, this Christ, but we never knew him until that moment of revelation and acceptance.

Oh, we may have known of him. But once we make him Lord and Savior of our life, we have truth. If we wander from the truth, and someone should bring us back, remember: *"Whoever turns a sinner from the error of his way will save him from death and cover over a multitude of sins."*

There have been times that I was the guy who has wandered off the trail, and I needed a brother to help me get back on track. Other times, I have had the privilege to help a believer back to the right road, the truth, and I get to see restoration take place. Again, in Matthew 18:12, Jesus uses the parable of the lost sheep to make a point of going after someone who has wandered off.

Matthew 18:12 *"What do you think? If a man owns a hundred sheep, and one of them wanders away, will he not leave the 99 on the hills and go look for the one that wandered off?"*

Here is the take-away from this: the sheep who has wandered off is the one who needs the attention, just as the man who wanders from the truth needs to be rescued and returned to the flock. The 99 are safe. The Good Sheppard cares for and wants all of His sheep in the safety of the flock. If one wanders away, his desire is to bring that sheep back to the closeness and protection of the good shepherd.

This restoration produces rejoicing when a man comes back to the truth, rejoins the flock, and realizes a new faith in the good shepherd, Jesus.

Here again is the wisdom of God. He shows us through Christ, his son, that Jesus is the shepherd who comes to our rescue. But he was also the Lamb of God, who takes away the sins of the world.

It is a high calling to be used of God. We will not, and could not, be the sacrifice, but we know the one who was. It should be an honor to help restore people who have wandered from the truth.

We are to assist our God, to reach the wandering sheep and bring them back to the good shepherd. Remember: "Whoever turns a sinner from the error of his way will save him from death and cover over a multitude of sins."

FINAL THOUGHTS

My heart is full. Dare I expect that this simple conversation with the half-brother of Jesus will launch us deep and wide into the faith we are called to walk in? Yes, there is power in simplicity.

We can walk the faith and not just talk the faith. When we do, we can continue to consider the trials and temptations we face as pure joy. My encouragement for all of us is to not let one precious day slip by without doing three things.

1- Communicate with the Father who loves you and who wants the very best for you.

2- Purpose to do at least one good deed for someone else, but not always the same person.

3- Give God all the praise, honor, and glory for everything, but not just the good things.

If we submit ourselves to Father God, we will not show favoritism, we will keep our mouth in check, and we will speak only words of encouragement. We will make the devil flee when we are strong in the spirit of God.

We will find patience in suffering and joy in the victory of overcoming. I hope you have enjoyed this brief conversation. I will continue to keep in my heart some of the things God has revealed through the short letter from James. I hope many conversations and observations have resulted from your reading.

May your life be a blessing to others as you are blessed by our Lord, and may these conversations continue as you search for the deeper things of God.

I think I am going to check out a guy named Peter. I heard that he wrote a letter and numbered it 1. See you there.

Many Blessings-

IN HIM

mel

ACKNOWELDGEMENTS

It has been a journey guided by the hand of God. This book you're holding became a reality, due to some God-ordained detours. I had actually started several projects prior to ***James & I & You***, and those will follow, but the Lord wanted this one first.

There are so many people who have put up with my dreaming, big ideas, failures, and success. Through the journey, they have been such an encouragement to me.

First and foremost, I must thank my Father. Father God, my one true dad. I am proud to be known as his kid.

Thank you, my beautiful wife, Maureen. You know my heart best and still love me most. Thank you for the encouragement and for giving me the space and grace to get this done.

Thank you to my five kids and their wonderful families. The grandkids always are a delight to papa's heart, and they put a smile on my face. Thank you for putting up with my silliness and for laughing at my bad jokes.

Thank you pastor Steve Dixon for your encouragement and support of our ministry.

Thank you to my partners in ministry and business for allowing me to grow in Christ.

Larry and Jan Robison, Marc King thank you for your encouragement. Thank you for the opportunity to work with people who really care.

Jack Ward, you are a true friend. It is a pleasure to get kingdom work done with you. Thank you for your encouragement and support.

Mark Howard, thank you for the encouragement and process to move this book and the ones to come forward.

Dave Plummer, one of my oldest friends, sooner or later we will do kingdom work together again.

Dale Armstrong, at Focus on the Family, for your friendship and encouragement.

To all the guys from the 2nd Saturday Men's Breakfast, and RealMen Ministries, Frank McDuffee, Mike Grean, and Jim Zalenski-"Runner" , Brian Center, Mike Smith, Art Nelson, Gary Webb, Marty Jordon, and Gary McLaughlin.

Thank you Bobby Howard and Brenda Bohannon who helped format this work, I am forever grateful.

And THANK YOU to the countless people who have touched my life and gave me encouragement when it was needed most. May the God of Peace return your kindness many times over.